Heroes Bomber Command
NORFOLK

Rupert Matthews

COUNTRYSIDE BOOKS
NEWBURY BERKSHIRE

First published 2006
© Rupert Matthews 2006

COUNTRYSIDE BOOKS
3 Catherine Road,
Newbury, Berkshire.

To view our complete range of books,
please visit us at
www.countrysidebooks.co.uk

ISBN 1 84674 000 2
EAN 978 184674 000 8

The cover picture shows the ground crew of a Mosquito of
No 105 Squadron at Marham, watching as another aircraft
swoops overhead.

Designed by Peter Davies, Nautilus Design
Produced through MRM Associates Ltd, Reading
Printed by Borcombe Printers plc, Romsey

CONTENTS

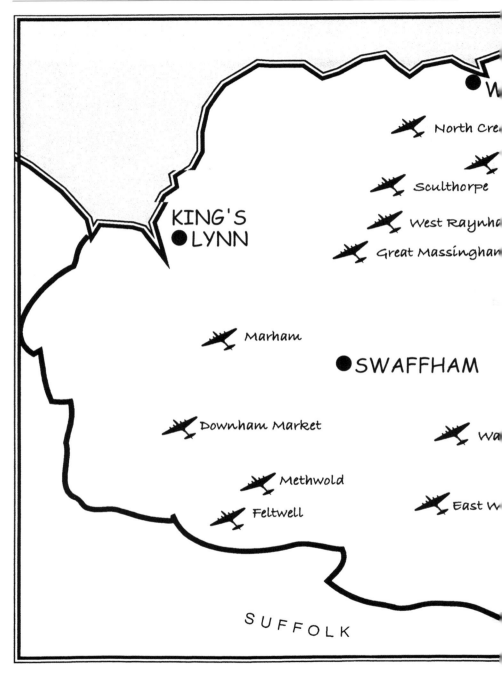

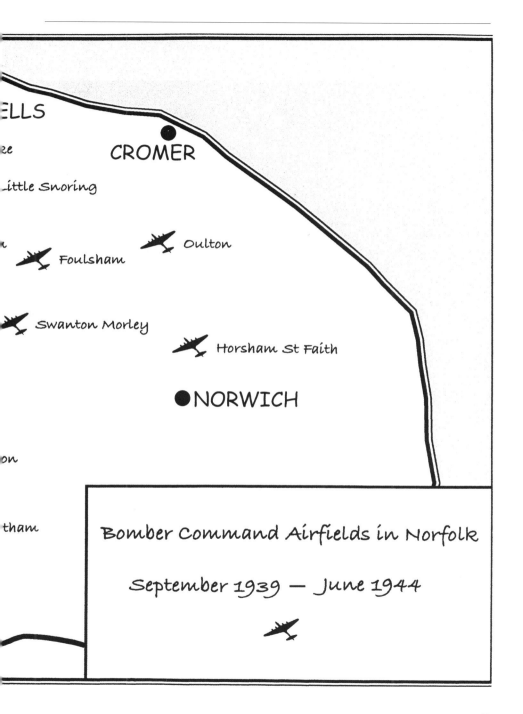

ELLS

2e

Little Snoring

CROMER

Foulsham

Oulton

Swanton Morley

Horsham St Faith

●NORWICH

on

tham

Bomber Command Airfields in Norfolk

September 1939 — June 1944

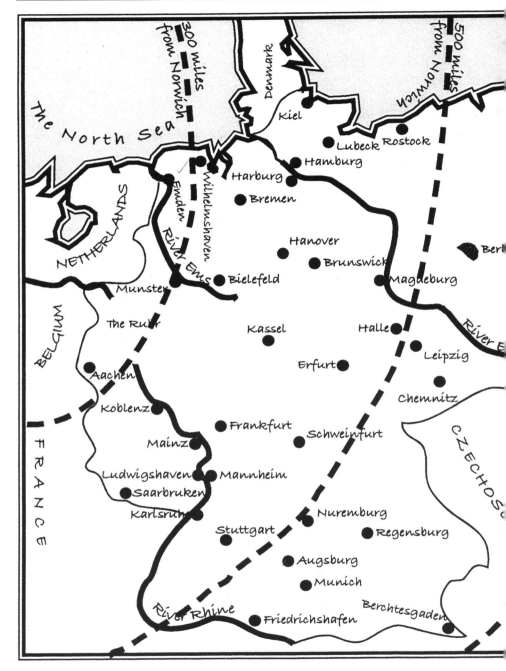

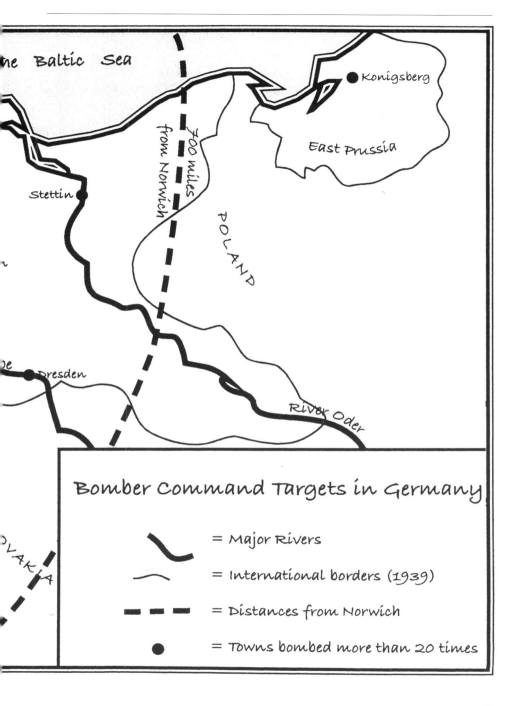

the Baltic Sea

Konigsberg

East Prussia

700 miles from Norwich

Stettin

POLAND

Dresden

River Oder

Bomber Command Targets in Germany

╲╱ = Major Rivers

∿ = International borders (1939)

▬ ▬ ▬ = Distances from Norwich

● = Towns bombed more than 20 times

VAKIA

Preface

Throughout my childhood I was aware, in a vague sort of a way, that my father had served with RAF Bomber Command during the Second World War. I knew that he had been stationed at a place called Swanton Morley in Norfolk, but not much else.

My father did not often talk about that period of his life. I knew that his squadron had flown Blenheims, but only because he helped me build an Airfix kit of a Blenheim IV. One of the few anecdotes about his time in Bomber Command that he shared with me when I was a boy concerned the small scar that he carried throughout his life.

One bright day in the autumn of 1940 Father was walking across the airfield to the sergeants' mess for lunch. As he passed a patch of grass, he saw a pair of workmen hacking at the ground, digging out a slit trench to give some protection to the squadron personnel in the event of an air raid. Lunch over, Father came out of the mess with a fellow sergeant and began to walk back towards the control tower. Suddenly Father's friend gripped him by the elbow and pointed off to the northeast.

'Look,' he said. 'That fellow's in trouble, his undercarriage is up. We'd better get back.'

Father followed the pointing finger to see a twin-engine aircraft approaching low and fast from the direction of the North Sea. Thinking it must be a Blenheim from another squadron coming in damaged for a crash landing, my father began to walk quickly back to his post. He glanced up again towards the aircraft and noticed something odd.

'What,' he asked his pal, 'are those funny red lights flashing on the wing?'

'Christ,' yelled his friend. 'He's shooting at us. It's a ruddy Jerry.'

Indeed, it was. Bombs began to burst on the airfield and the grass leapt and danced as machine gun bullets tore up the ground. With little time to act, my father spotted the slit trench that he had seen beginning to be dug not quite an hour earlier. Thinking the workmen would not have had time to do much, he leapt into it head first. To his horror he saw that the trench was well over six feet deep. The last thing he saw before he blacked out was a spade and pickaxe rushing up to meet him.

When Father came to, the German aircraft had gone. The airfield personnel were racing around to collect the wounded, repair the runway and douse the fires. Looking down at himself, my father found blood splattered liberally around. His head was barely scratched, but his hand had caught badly on the sharp blade of the shovel and been sliced deeply open.

As war wounds go, it was nothing very spectacular. But to my boyhood mind it made my father a genuine war hero. And in his way, I suppose, he was.

As to why my father never really said much about his time in the RAF, I found that out when I grew older. My father had lost a lot of friends in the war. I recall he told me of the many times he stood by the control tower waiting for aircraft that would never return. He sounded very upset, even then in the 1980s. And a pair of flying boots that I fondly thought to have been my father's had in fact belonged to a particular pal of his who had been shot down and killed. Father kept them to his dying day, and now I keep them.

So for my father, for his pals – whether they returned or not – and for all the others who served in Bomber Command, I am proud to write this book.

As the title suggests, the main subjects are the men who fought in Bomber Command in Norfolk during the war. For those readers with a wider interest in the RAF who want to learn more about Fighter Command or Coastal Command as well as about the airfields and unit histories I can do no better than advise you to purchase *Norfolk Airfields in the Second World War* by Graham Smith, also published by Countryside Books, which makes a fine companion volume to this.

Of course, such a book cannot possibly be the work of just one person. I would particularly like to thank Flight Lieutenant Andrew Smith for his help in making contact with various serving and retired officers and men of the RAF. I would like to thank Antony Robinson of the Massingham Historical Society's Sister Laurence RAF Massingham Museum for all his help and for giving me permission to reproduce photographs and documents from his archives, credited in the text as *Massingham MHSSLRAFMM*. Acknowledgments must also go to Paul Garland of the Feltwell Society for permission to draw on his archives. The Feltwell Society can be contacted through their website: www.feltwell.org/index.htm. The operational base of RAF Marham has a magnificent History Room, and I would like to thank the RAF for permission to draw on it for illustrations. I must also thank the staff of Darby Nursery Stock Ltd who were kind enough to help me when I got lost trying to find the site of RAF Methwold – and all the others who gave me directions or helped in other ways. I would also like to thank Shaun

Smith, a retired RAF officer, for the use of his fine library of photographs of RAF-related sites and memorials. He can be emailed on spikesmith@clara. net and is happy to provide copies of his photographs for a small charge. I would also like to thank Abigail King for her help with the research. Finally, I would thank my father for his inspiration and my wife for her patience.

The Lancaster Bomber Just Jane *is preserved at East Kirby airfield.*
(www.oldairfields.fotopic.net)

Introduction

Norfolk was to become one of the most important counties used by Bomber Command during the Second World War, but it had not always been so. Indeed, at first Norfolk had barely registered with the RAF at all.

In 1919 the British government adopted a stance known as 'the Ten Year Rule', to which it still largely adheres. Put simply, this restricted the Ministry of War (Defence, as it is now) to preparing only for conflicts that the Foreign Office thought possible within the next ten years. In 1919 the Great War was barely over. Nobody thought another major European war likely. As a consequence the RAF was instructed to prepare only for minor wars fought far from home in the further reaches of the Empire.

The RAF was fortunate at this time to have as its commander Sir Hugh Trenchard, who had fought through the Great War and was a firm believer in air power as a war-winning weapon. Trenchard's room for action was severely limited by the Ten Year Rule, which effectively halted the production of modern war aircraft. However, he put his formidable organisational talents to work on the manpower of the RAF. He established the Service as a professional core onto which a later expansion could be built. What money could be spared for new technology went on developing fast bombers. By the time Trenchard left the RAF in 1929 the shape of the future force was clear, if masked by antiquated biplanes.

It was in 1933 that the Ten Year Rule first allowed for the possibility of a major European war, with Germany as the most likely enemy. It was at this point that the RAF came to Norfolk. Marham and Feltwell were designated as bomber stations and construction work began.

At this date the aircraft were still antiquated 'stringbags'. The Handley Page Heyford was one of the best of these. By 1935 no fewer than eleven squadrons were equipped with Heyfords. These lumbering twin-engine biplanes had an odd configuration with the fuselage attached to the upper wing, and the lower wing being entirely separate from the rest of the airframe. The Heyford would remain in service with front line squadrons until the spring of 1939 and retained a role as a trainer until 1943.

Even as the Heyford entered service, it was recognised that it was already obsolete when compared with the daring monoplane designs being produced by the Germans. In 1934 and 1935 the RAF issued a series of specifications for two- and four-engined bombers to the aircraft industry. Meanwhile,

*A Heyford bomber, last of the bi-plane bombers to serve in RAF Bomber Command.
It was still in service just a few months before the Second World War began.*

*A Fairey Hendon of No 38 Squadron parked on the grass at RAF Marham in 1938.
The Hendon was the RAF's first metal monoplane bomber with internal bomb bay
and guns in enclosed turrets. It was withdrawn from front line service in July 1939.*

orders were made for modern transport aircraft to be rapidly adapted for use as bombers. The results were the Handley Page Harrow and the Fairey Hendon. The Hendon was phased out by the summer of 1939, but the Harrow was still in front line service in Norfolk when the war broke out.

In 1936 the government finally agreed to a massive build up in the services as war became increasingly likely. The RAF was allowed to order modern aircraft in large numbers, and the aircraft industry was told that military orders were to take priority over civilian work. So far as the Norfolk stations were concerned, this meant the arrival of two new aircraft types: the Blenheim and the Wellington. Between them these two types would equip all front line Norfolk squadrons by mid-September 1939.

Meanwhile, the RAF itself was reorganised. On 14 July 1936 Bomber Command was born at Hillingdon House, RAF Uxbridge. By July 1937 the new Command had been divided into six Groups, numbered 1 to 6. Each Group covered a geographic area. Norfolk at this date fell under

A Harrow parked beside a hangar at RAF Marham in 1938. Unlike the gunners aboard the Hendon bombers, those serving in Harrows had to cope without enclosed positions, making their job a chilly one.

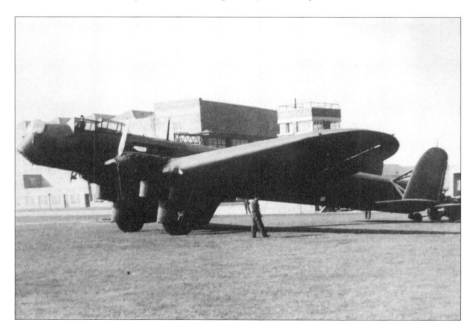

No 3 Group. At Feltwell were No 37 and No 214 Squadrons, both flying Harrows. Marham was the base for No 38 Squadron, which had Heyfords, and for No 115 Squadron, which flew Hendons.

In September 1938, Hitler engineered the 'Munich Crisis' with his insistent and urgent demands that border areas of Czechoslovakia inhabited mostly by ethnic Germans should be handed over to Germany. For a few tense weeks it looked as if hostilities might break out. On 10 September the government ordered total mobilisation for war. It proved to be a depressing time for Bomber Command. Of the 57 squadrons, 15 could not mobilise due to a lack of aircraft, ten had Harrows which were widely recognised as being obsolete and the rest managed on average to get only 50% of their paper strength ready for action.

The head of Bomber Command at the time was Sir Edgar Ludlow-Hewitt, often referred to simply as Ludlow. Analysing what had gone wrong, Ludlow recognised serious deficiencies in the infrastructure of airfields and supply bases as well as poor staff training and a lack of crews prepared properly for operational duties. He began a crash programme of reorganisation with 5 August 1939 as his deadline.

In Norfolk, Watton and West Raynham airfields were brought into service, with Nos 21 and 82 Squadrons flying out of Watton and No 101 Squadron out of West Raynham, all equipped with Blenheims. These two bases fell under No 2 Group. Meanwhile, No 3 Group operated No 37 Squadron out of Feltwell, Nos 38 and 115 Squadrons out of Marham and No 214 out of Methwold, all with Wellington bombers.

Over a period of six days beginning on 5 August, Ludlow held his practice mobilisation. Squadrons were sent to attack dummy targets in Britain and in France. Group HQ staff were put through their paces organising supply systems, identifying targets and coping with 'losses'. Air defences were forced to cope with dummy attacks by 'enemy' aircraft. The results were mixed. Generally the support and staff sections performed well, but only 40% of aircraft managed to find their targets.

Ludlow realised that there was much work still to be done. But time was running out. On 3 September 1939 Britain went to war with Germany.

Handley Page Harrow

Type:	Medium bomber
Engines:	2 x 925 hp Bristol Pegasus XX
Wingspan:	88 ft 5 in
Length:	82 ft 2 in
Height:	19 ft 5 in
Weight:	Empty 13,600 lb Loaded 23,000 lb
Armament:	4 x 0.303 in machine guns in nose, dorsal and tail turrets
Bomb-load:	3,000 lb of bombs
Max speed:	200 mph
Ceiling:	22,800 ft
Range:	1,840 miles
Production:	100

The Harrow was a stopgap measure produced by converting the Handley Page HP-51 transport aircraft into a bomber. It entered service with the RAF in February 1937, but already production was being wound down as the more advanced Hampden was approved for service and production. A few squadrons still had Harrows when war broke out, but these were immediately taken out of front line service and redesignated as training units. By 1940 all Harrows had been converted back to being transports, in which role they spent the rest of the war. Harrows were still on active service with the RAF in May 1945, though only five were in flying condition.

An advert by the Handley Page company in a popular magazine. In the run-up to war, several companies placed similar advertisements extolling their part in the rearmament programme.

War Comes to Norfolk

A Wellington bomber flies over RAF Marham in August 1939, just days before war was declared.

Even **before war broke out,** RAF Bomber Command in Norfolk was preparing for conflict. On 26 August 1939 telegrams were sent to all personnel not on base ordering their immediate return. On the same day aircraft were dispersed around the airfield perimeters in case of sudden Luftwaffe attacks.

On 1 September, War Plan 7b was issued to Bomber Command. This restricted bombers to attacking purely military targets so that there was no risk whatever of causing civilian casualties. In practice this meant that only ships at sea or in naval docks could be attacked, all army and Luftwaffe bases being too close to civilian areas to be certain that only military personnel would be killed. Bomber crews were told that they could fly over Germany, but only for reconnaissance purposes or to drop leaflets.

The policy was not popular, but it was practical. As Commander-in-Chief of Bomber Command, Ludlow was worried that his aircraft were unable to penetrate deep into enemy territory with any degree of safety. And the French were terrified that any German civilian casualties would result in massive Luftwaffe raids on French cities – which would be much easier for the Germans to reach than British targets.

The first few weeks of war were quiet ones for Bomber Command in Norfolk. Nos 214 and 101 Squadrons were stood down to Reserve status as soon as war was declared. Although other squadrons remained active, they took no part in the early attacks on German naval ships that occupied other units in both No 2 Group and No 3 Group. That changed dramatically on 3 December, when a strong force of 24 Wellingtons drawn from Nos 38, 115 and 149 Squadrons, the former two operating from Marham, took off on a seek and destroy sortie across the coastal waters off Germany.

The Wellingtons flew in the pre-war approved tight formation at medium height. Off Heligoland Island the force sighted a pair of German cruisers and raced in to the attack. Most bombs missed their target and those that hit inflicted negligible damage. One wide miss hit Heligoland itself. Although the bomb fell harmlessly onto open fields, it caused a stir as it was the first to explode on German soil in the war.

Meanwhile, the formation of bombers was coming under attack from a swarm of Messerschmitt Bf 109 and Bf 110 fighters. The Germans kept warily away from the British defensive machine guns, but a long range burst damaged the starboard wing and rudder of the No 38 Squadron Wellington flown by Sergeant O'Doire. The aircraft veered off course and left the protective formation of bombers. At once a Bf 109 dived in for the

An unidentified wounded Flight Sergeant is presented with the Distinguished Flying Medal at a parade at RAF Marham in June 1940.

kill. The German pilot approached from below and behind, holding his fire until he was just 40 yards from the Wellington. At the same moment that the German opened fire, Aircraftsman John Copley in the rear turret of the Wellington let loose a burst of 20 rounds. The Messerschmitt was hit and climbed steeply, exposing its underbelly to the delighted Copley, who poured in a long burst of fire. The Messerschmitt stalled, turned on its back and dived into the sea.

Aircraftsman Copley was awarded a Distinguished Flying Medal (DFM) for the action, but his success had the unfortunate effect of convincing several senior officers that modern bombers, protected by machine guns in powered turrets, could ward off fighters. It would take some months, and the loss of many men, before minds were changed.

On 18 December ten out of 22 Wellingtons from No 3 Group were shot down by German fighters attacking from above and to the side. The losses were put down to poor formation-keeping by the dead pilots rather than to the vulnerability of bombers to this sort of attack. A run of bad weather in January and February 1940 brought an end to the large scale formation sweeps, and thus an end to heavy losses. Lone aircraft flying out of Norfolk still undertook patrols, as bombers from other areas were dropping leaflets across Germany, but it was not until March that operations could begin again in earnest.

On 11 March one of these patrols over the North Sea led to a most unexpected result. Squadron Leader Miles Delap was flying a Blenheim of No 82 Squadron from Watton to reconnoitre German naval shipping around Kiel, when he emerged from low cloud off Borkum. Right in front of the aircraft was a U-boat on the surface. Delap hurriedly attacked, managing to drop four bombs from a height of just 500 feet. Two of the bombs hit the U-boat, which sank immediately with no survivors. The victim turned out to be U-31, a Type VIIA Atlantic raider. The Blenheim suffered a degree of damage to its undercarriage caused by the bomb blasts, but Squadron Leader Delap continued with the reconnaissance mission before returning home. His navigator was Sergeant Robert Wyness, who would later become one of the best air photographers of the war, being awarded the DFM for his work.

On 2 April Bomber Command received a new Commander-in-Chief in the shape of Air Marshal Sir Charles Portal. Ludlow had been due to be replaced some months earlier and only the pressing demands of war had persuaded the Air Ministry to keep him in post. He had done a magnificent job of reorganising Bomber Command for war, but there was a feeling among some in the government that he was too cautious when it came to risking his new force in battle. Portal was considered more of a fighting officer. It was not long before he got a chance to prove himself.

On 9 April Germany invaded Denmark and Norway without warning and with barely the courtesy of declaring war. Denmark surrendered almost at once, but King Haakon of Norway decided to fight. Britain and France, of course, moved swiftly to help their new ally against Germany. The men of Norfolk's squadrons were immediately in the thick of it.

On the same day as the German invasion, No 115 Squadron was sent to attack German warships off the Norwegian coast. All six aircraft that took part were hit by anti-aircraft fire. Four were fitted with new self-sealing fuel tanks and escaped unscathed, but the two that had the older fuel tanks both caught fire and crashed with no survivors. Aircraft without self-sealing

A statue of Air Marshal Sir Charles Portal, who became head of Bomber Command in April 1940. This statue stands outside the Ministry of Defence in London.

A reconnaissance photograph of Stavanger airfield taken in preparation for the raid by Nos 37 and 115 Squadrons. Key: (1) Runways; (2) German aircraft that have collided; (3) German aircraft with broken wing; and (4) Stacks of stores.

tanks were quickly relegated to training or to reserve uses.

On 11 April No 115 Squadron was again sent to Norway, this time to bomb Stavanger airfield, which had been seized by the Germans and was being used as a base for their own bombing operations. The squadron's aircraft were flown to Kinloss in Scotland for refuelling before the raid. It was decided to attack from a height of 300 feet, approaching from the sea out of the setting sun in the hope of evading German spotters.

The second aircraft in the leading section was piloted by Flight Sergeant Gordon Powell. As the Wellingtons tore over the airfield perimeter, a battery of pom-pom guns opened up. Instantly the lead aircraft disappeared in a ball of orange flame. Powell's was now the leading aircraft. He dropped his bombs on the runway and was then hit almost simultaneously by three pom-pom shells. The first exploded just beneath the tail of the aircraft, wounding the rear gunner. The second exploded above the bomb bay, but did little damage. The third struck the cockpit, injuring Powell in the left shoulder and destroying the hydraulic system.

Despite his injuries, Flight Sergeant Powell dived down to ground level and turned his Wellington out to sea. It was flying nose down and the controls were very sluggish due to the damage caused to the tail. He dragged the aircraft up to a relatively safe height while his crew surveyed the damage and patched up the wounds of the rear gunner. Only then did he reveal his own injuries and hand over to the second pilot while they were dressed. The second pilot, however, was quite inexperienced at night flying so Powell took over the controls again. After a nerve-racking flight of almost 400 miles over the North Sea, he sighted Kinloss. Without hydraulics the undercarriage would not lock down, so he was faced with a crash landing. He managed to put his Wellington down without injury to the crew, though the aircraft had to be written off.

Another aircraft from No 115 Squadron on the same raid ran into trouble on its way home when the wireless suddenly stopped working. The radio operator, Leading Aircraftsman Graham Smith, almost took it to pieces trying to trace the fault, but without success. Once back on the ground the radio worked perfectly. The aircraft was cleared by the ground staff as fit

The burnt out wreck of a No 37 Squadron Wellington at RAF Feltwell in March 1940. The aircraft was being bombed-up for a raid when an armourer noticed a fault with a photoflash bomb. He just had time to alert his comrades before the bomb went off, triggering the rest of the load and destroying the aircraft.

for operations, but Smith refused point blank to accept that nothing was wrong. The radio was inspected again, and again nothing was found. The commanding officer began to wonder if the 18 year old was trying to avoid combat, but on the third attempt the ground crew, with Smith helping, identified the problem as being a hairline fracture of a valve that was invisible except with the use of a magnifying glass. Leading Aircraftsman Smith was vindicated, and went on to be one of the most valued and skilful electronics experts in Bomber Command. He later served with the Pathfinders and completed 72 operational missions.

Joining No 115 Squadron on the Stavanger raid were a number of Wellingtons of No 37 Squadron out of Feltwell. Both the commander and his deputy were shot down over the airfield. It was left to the next senior officer, Sydney Snowden, to gather the remaining aircraft, most of which were damaged, and lead them back to base.

By the end of April the Germans had conquered southern Norway. Attempts were made by the Allies to hold on to Narvik in the far north, but this was out of range of Bomber Command. For the squadrons of Norfolk, the Norwegian campaign was over. A new and deadlier one was about to begin.

On 10 May 1940 the German panzers surged forward into Belgium and the Netherlands. The British and French armies marched to meet them, but the German attack was a feint. The main armoured thrust was launched further south through the Ardennes. Within a week it was clear that the Allied armies were in serious danger of being cut off and destroyed. The need to halt the German advance was paramount.

Unfortunately the attack had been preceded by massed Luftwaffe raids on French airfields which effectively rendered the French Air Force useless. Norfolk's bomber squadrons were called on to do their bit. At first Air Marshal Portal was against the move. His men and aircraft, he argued, were trained and armed for attacks on ships or on factories – not on troops, supply convoys and other moving land targets. Portal was overruled.

On 14 May No 115 Squadron was sent at night to attack a German road convoy near Hirson. By the time the bombers arrived, the trucks had gone. Flying Officer Oliver Donaldson turned away to head back home and at once came under heavy anti-aircraft fire from a nearby wood. Reasoning the fire must be defending something, he dropped his bombs on the wood. A massive explosion, followed by at least twelve others, tore through the forest. Donaldson had hit and destroyed a major ammunition store.

These attacks on the advancing German armies proved to be very costly. One Wellington of No 115 Squadron was shot down, only the navigator, Sergeant Ronald Lambert, parachuting to safety. Evacuated through Dunkirk, Lambert returned to Marham and immediately volunteered to take the place of a wounded navigator with another crew. In less than two weeks he was back in action over France.

In No 115 Squadron, Flying Officer Donaldson's crew was one of the few pre-war crews to survive to the end of June, by which time they had undertaken 19 night raids over France as well as numerous sweeps across the North Sea. The navigator, Raymond Stowe, later took great pains to train up replacement navigators to a standard at which they might survive the dangers of combat. 'His courage and efficiency played no small part in the speed with which this unit recovered from the heavy losses of May-June,' recorded the squadron commander. Such steady, reliable courage was highly valued in the RAF, and rightly so.

A poster in the RAF Marham History Room displays the badge of the station. The station began life as a Royal Flying Corps airfield in the First World War, then spent most of the interwar years mothballed until it was reopened in 1937. Marham is still an operational base, the oldest in Norfolk.

The efforts of Bomber Command, impressive though they were, failed to halt the overwhelming might of the German panzers. On 20 May the Germans reached the sea at Abbeville. The entire British army and much of the main French force were now cut off in Belgium and northern France. The British began their retreat to Dunkirk, the only Channel port left available for an evacuation by sea. On 26 May the first troops were evacuated from the beaches by the Royal Navy. Bomber Command was ordered to support the evacuation by attacking the German army and its supply lines.

Typical was the attack carried out at night by No 115 Squadron with its Wellingtons. On 21 May it was sent to attack a concentration of panzers south of Dunkirk. The target could not be found, so the Wellingtons dropped their bombs in an attempt to destroy a bridge, then went down low to machine gun the enemy lines. Aircraftsman Thomas Moir was shot through the foot as he used his rear turret guns to shoot up a battery of guns. Despite the agony of shattered bones, he remained at his post all the way home, but fainted from loss of blood within seconds of landing.

Not that Air Marshal Portal had given up entirely on his preferred targets. He managed to argue the case that railway junctions and oil refineries inside Germany were crucial to the advance of the German armies in France, and so was allowed to send forces to bomb them.

On 18 June No 38 Squadron was sent to attack the mainline railway junction near Bremen. On arrival the target was found to be protected by barrage balloons, searchlights and heavy anti-aircraft fire. Undeterred, Sergeant John Gibbs dived down to below 7,000 feet, weaved between the balloons and plastered the rail lines with explosives, setting one train on fire.

It should not be thought that all raids went successfully, even when enemy action did not get in the way. On 15 May nine aircraft from No 37 Squadron took off from Feltwell to attack the oil plant at Holten. A bank of cloud masked the coast, causing eight of the nine aircraft to lose their way.

Aircrew of No 38 Squadron pose in front of a Wellington bomber. Note the single machine gun protruding from a slot in the nose rather than the more usual twin gun turret, making this a Mk1C.

The only bomber to find the target was that piloted by Sergeant George Watt, part of a crew which consistently found targets at night and bombed accurately. It was becoming increasingly obvious that navigating at night over blacked out territory was extremely difficult.

One of the aircraft to lose their way was the Wellington in which Aircraftsman Charles Dear served as wireless operator. Dear later recalled:

'On arrival in the target area we began a low-level search for the works we were to bomb. Suddenly a searchlight latched on to us and 'Darky' Stanhope in the rear turret opened fire on it. He did not hit the light but must have scared its crew since the light ceased to follow us but remained stationary and pointing straight up. Strangely there was no gunfire aimed at us. We continued our search without success. Even at low level it was difficult to find one's way about in the dark. Eventually we stumbled across an autobahn and decided to bomb it. A very accurate low-level run was made down it and bombs released and we could feel the concussion when the bombs exploded. Shortly afterwards the air turned blue when we flew over a fairly large factory and we had nothing left to throw at it.'

Another crew able to achieve consistent success belonged to No 82 Squadron at Watton and had Sergeant Harold Bareham as navigator. 'He is an exceptional navigator who has successfully led the formation direct to the target on every one of 23 operational flights,' wrote his squadron commander in July 1940. But Sergeant Bareham's most famous triumph came the night of 11 July. After successfully finding and attacking an oil plant near Bremen, his aircraft was hit by flak. A large portion of the side of the Blenheim was blown off, and the resulting tornado of wind blasted away all the maps and other equipment that Bareham was using. Undeterred, he peered out of the hole in the side of his aircraft at the stars. By dead reckoning he managed to guide the aircraft back to base with unerring accuracy.

Improvements to navigational equipment were clearly needed, but in the summer of 1940 not even the most pessimistic of RAF commanders realised the true extent of the difficulties. And before anything could be done about night navigation, a far more pressing problem presented itself. When France surrendered to Germany on 22 June, Britain was left alone. The vast German army stood poised to invade across the English Channel.

The Battle of Britain was about to begin. And the men of Bomber Command in Norfolk found themselves in the front line.

Vickers Wellington

Type:	Medium bomber
Engines:	Mk I 2 x 1050 hp
	Bristol Pegasus XVIII
	Mk II 2 x 1145 hp
	Rolls-Royce Merlin X
	Mk III 1500 hp Bristol
	Hercules XI
Wingspan:	86 ft 2 in
Length:	64 ft 7 in
Height:	17 ft 5 in
Weight:	Empty 18,556 lb
	Loaded 29,500 lb
Armament:	6 (later 8) x 0.303 in machine guns in nose turret, tail turret and side windows
Bomb-load:	4,500 lb of bombs, or one mine or one torpedo
Max speed:	255 mph
Ceiling:	19,000 ft
Range:	2,200 miles
Production:	11,462

The Wellington was designed by the aircraft genius Barnes Wallis, later responsible for the bouncing bomb and other innovations. The most noticeable feature of the bomber was its astonishingly robust design which allowed Wellingtons to fly safely home even when missing sections of wing or tail and with gaping holes in the fuselage. The strength was due to the geodetic framing devised by Barnes Wallis, though this flexible structure gave inexperienced crews frights as the wings wobbled alarmingly in flight. The Wellington entered service with the RAF in October 1938 and by December 1941 it comprised half the strength of Bomber Command, equipping 21 squadrons. As the new heavier bombers were brought into the bombing campaign against Germany, Wellingtons were moved to the Mediterranean and Far East theatres where they continued in service right to the end of the war.

Chapter 2

Invasion Alert!

By **June of 1940** half of the operational strength Bomber Command had possessed at the outbreak of war had been lost. Casualties had been highest among those squadrons sent to France, and some of these would soon be based in Norfolk, but the squadrons already operating out of the county had also lost their share of men and aircraft.

With this reduced force, Air Marshal Sir Charles Portal, Commander-in-Chief of Bomber Command, had to face a suddenly increased workload. On 4 June the government instructed him to give top priority to destroying German oil storage and refining plants. Two weeks later this policy was changed to direct the bombers toward aircraft factories, these by then being recognised as vital to the Luftwaffe's efforts to win the Battle of Britain. On 4 July, Portal was told that a German invasion of Britain was considered imminent and ordered to send his bombers to attack German shipping and transportation barges, as well as enemy-held ports. Just nine days later he was ordered to switch back to attacking oil plants and aircraft factories.

Faced by such contradictory orders, Portal protested that he and his men needed clear and consistent instructions if they were to stand any chance of planning and executing useful raids. Pending such a luxury, he decided to launch his aircraft against whichever target suited them best. For Norfolk, this meant that the shorter range Blenheims were sent against shipping and targets close to the coast of occupied Europe. Very often these involved

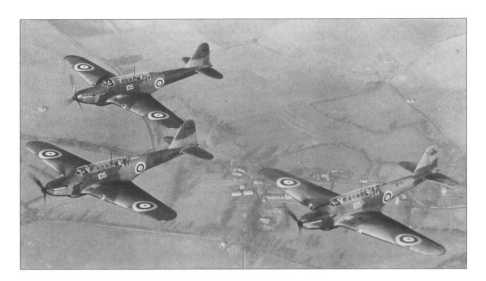

A flight of Fairey Battles. When the survivors of the Advance Air Striking Force that had fought in France arrived in Norfolk they were equipped with these light bombers that had proven to be so ineffective in combat against the German Luftwaffe.

attacks on defended ports or on the growing concentrations of barges in various rivers that the Germans obviously intended to use in the expected invasion of Britain. The Wellingtons, with their longer range and heavier bomb-load, were sent to targets in Germany itself. These sorties were directed against individual armaments factories or oil works on the rather optimistic assumption that the crews could find such targets at night after a long flight in darkness.

That such faith was often misplaced was shown by the plight of the Wellington in which flew Aircraftsman Charles Dear, who later recalled:

'On 3 August we set out for Gelsenkirchen, but unable to find our target we returned to Feltwell with our bombs still on board only to find the airfield fogbound and we were unable to land. I cannot recall if any diversion system was in being at that time, I suspect not. I do remember that we proceeded aimlessly inland with the hope of finding somewhere to land. On reaching the Midlands we found some hilltops poking up through the fog and circled these while considering whether to drop the bombs 'safe' and then crash land alongside. It was while doing so that we stumbled across an airfield, which proved to be the training school at Desford, near Leicester. Unfortunately all sorts of obstructions had been placed on it as an anti-invasion measure but we saw that a narrow strip had been left clear alongside a hedge, probably unintentionally. It was on this strip that we managed a safe landing much to the amazement of the Station Commander and his staff, particularly when they saw the bomb load on board. In the meantime I had failed to wind in my trailing aerial, the lead weights of which must have cracked a few roof tiles during the course of our approach for landing.'

One of the few pilots who unequivocally did find his target was Flight Lieutenant Patrick Lynch-Blosse of No 115 Squadron, who in August 1940 flew out of Marham in his Wellington to attack an aircraft factory in Bernberg. Having been uncertain on some earlier raids whether or not he had actually hit his target, Lynch-Blosse dived down to a height of just 3,000 feet. He found that he was not over the intended factory, so pulled up, aimed again and dived down, this time to 2,000 feet. Surrounded by flak, he dropped his bombs with deadly accuracy and set the factory alight. Other No 115 Squadron aircraft then bombed the fires, reducing the factory to rubble.

There were, of course, problems associated with low-level bombing. When coming in at around 1,000 feet to ensure accurate bombing of the docks at Flushing, Pilot Officer Frank Denton of No 75 Squadron released the bombs accurately, only for his Wellington to be catapulted several hundred feet up into the air when what must have been an ammunition dump exploded in a sheet of flame. Denton had to wrestle with the controls for some seconds to get the aircraft back on an even keel. His observer nervously reported that a hole had been blown straight through the starboard wing, while the port wing had lost some four feet off its tip. Fortunately the Wellington lived up to its rugged reputation and made it back to Feltwell safely.

Not that losing the way was always a problem. On 18 July No 75 Squadron navigator Sergeant William Allinson got lost somewhere over Germany. Giving up all hope of finding their designated target, Allinson told his pilot to attack the first thing he saw. This turned out to be a train sitting stationary in a siding. The Wellington bombed with precision, causing a massive fire which indicated that the train had been carrying fuel. The flames could be seen by the tail gunner even when the rapidly retreating aircraft was some 40 miles away from the scene of the attack.

The attacks on coastal targets were no less hazardous for the Blenheim crews. On 19 August No 101 Squadron sent out a force to attack Antwerp airfield. As the aircraft crossed the coast, that flown by Pilot Officer Nigel

Bicknell had its port engine suddenly cut out. Rather than turn for home, Bicknell peeled off to attack the nearby Haamstad Luftwaffe base. The remaining engine was damaged in the attack, forcing him to put the bomber down into the North Sea, though he did manage to find a British trawler first. The gunner was killed in the landing, and Bicknell suffered head injuries. The observer, William Gingell, dragged Bicknell into the emergency raft before he passed out due to his own injuries. The two unconscious men were rescued by the trawler a few minutes later and ultimately returned to duty.

Even when base was reached, a crew's trials were not always over, as recalled by Ben Bussey of No 115 Squadron when talking about an incident in August 1940. The Wellington in which he was second pilot was hit by flak and lost all hydraulic controls:

'The Wellington would normally land at approximately 90 mph and we were coming in at about 120 mph with no flap control, brakes etc. We hit the ground and just went on and on until we struck a Nissen-type hut, a small brick construction which the Pioneer Corps used as a cookhouse, then we hit a Crossley lorry which had a Lewis gun mounted on it for aerodrome defence, then an air-raid bunker before tangling in the barbed wire surrounding the aerodrome which brought us to a halt. We finished up not far from a farmhouse and I remember the petrol running down the ploughed field all in flames. The pilot ran from the aircraft which was now well alight as did I, after I had kicked out a panel at the rear end.

'It was then I remembered my mate Pete Mcurrie who was in the front turret. I ran back and could see him shouting to me but I couldn't hear him. I got in and opened the turret doors and he said, "My legs are jammed, I can't move." I pulled him but it was no good. By this time the crash team had arrived but couldn't reach us because of the barbed wire. I called for an axe and someone hurled one across. It seemed to be in the air forever but I eventually got it and managed to free my buddy from the blazing Wellington. By this time the rescue team had got through the wire and took us both to the ambulance where a gruff voice told me to get in although I had said I was OK.

'On arriving at the sick bay the doctor's first words were, "How is your sister?" and much to my surprise it was our family doctor, Dr Monroe from Northwold, he was a Flight Lieutenant. I never met up with Pete Mcurrie again although I did visit his home at Cleveleys near Blackpool and his father told me he was still in hospital so he took me to his club and bought me a pint or two.'

On 30 September, Portal at last got specific settled orders. The invasion threat, he was informed, was over. Attacks on the invasion fleet and its communications could cease. Instead, Bomber Command was to concentrate on industrial and economic targets inside Germany. Portal's first move was to order the establishment of a Photographic Reconnaissance Unit (PRU) and give it the task of taking 'before and after' photographs of raid targets. Portal was becoming increasingly worried about the accuracy of raids. His second move, on 4 October, was to relinquish command of Bomber Command. He was promoted to be Chief of the Air Staff, a post he was to hold for the rest of the war.

Portal's place as Commander-in-Chief was taken by Air Chief Marshal Sir Richard Peirse, an experienced staff officer. Peirse inherited orders to bomb factories, oil targets and other economic targets in Germany. He also inherited a growing force that was by November 1940 back up to its September 1939 strength.

There had been some concern that the new airmen being trained up would not match the standard of pre-war professionals. This was particularly a concern when it came to men drawn from the colonies. Peirse need not have worried, as an exploit by the crew of 'M Mother' of New Zealand's No 75 Squadron showed early in October. While over the Ruhr, Pilot Officer Duncan McArthur spotted an aircraft in the dark which fired a series of coloured flares. Reasoning this must be a Luftwaffe nightfighter identifying itself to the flak crews below, McArthur edged his Wellington alongside the dark shape. The aircraft was identified as a Messerschmitt Bf 110, so front gunner Sergeant John Mylod raked it with gunfire, sending the German

No 75 Squadron was formed at Feltwell in April 1940, almost exclusively from New Zealand servicemen. The unit soon made a name for itself attacking German forces as they invaded Denmark and Norway.

A propaganda postcard issued in the autumn of 1940. As was typical of this period the aircraft of Fighter Command are featured prominently while Bomber Command does not even rate a mention. Despite the vital and dangerous work performed by Bomber Command attacking German invasion barges and troops, they got little recognition – a source of endless frustration to the men of bomber squadrons that still rankled decades after the war ended.

down in flames. It was a rare case of a bomber downing a nightfighter over Germany.

Less fortunate was the Wellington of No 115 Squadron sent to attack a factory near Berlin on 14 November. Over the target a flak shell knocked out the starboard engine. The wireless operator, Sergeant Howard Cleverley at once sent out the standard signal to Marham indicating that damage had been sustained. An hour later it became clear that the aircraft was in serious trouble. Cleverley again followed textbook procedure by asking Marham to provide him with a direction finding (DF) radio fix, by means of which he was able to establish his position accurately and keep it constantly updated. Over the North Sea, the second engine cut out. Sergeant Cleverley signalled Marham with the aircraft's position even as it began its glide down to the sea.

The pilot, Sergeant Harry Morson, splashed the aircraft down successfully, the entire crew managing to scramble into the emergency dinghy. Less than three hours later a destroyer picked them up. Sergeant Cleverley's use of the radio was later given as an example to other wireless operators as to how they should behave in similar circumstances.

In December 1940 several weeks of atrocious weather settled over Europe, making strategic bombing raids almost impossible. Peirse put the time to good use training his crews and building up the strength of Bomber Command.

One man who went through his training at this time was a young pilot named Arthur Ashworth, later to become a Wing Commander. He recalled:

'At the end of January 1941 I joined No 75 (New Zealand) Squadron at Feltwell having only once seen the inside of a Wellington. It wasn't until midway through February that I flew my first solo after two and a quarter hours dual. Shortly afterwards I was off, as a second pilot, on my first operational flight. I wasn't particularly apprehensive about this until I saw enemy flak coming up for the first time and suddenly realised that it was possibly intended for me! There were ten more trips as second pilot before I was given my own crew. I had also spent a considerable time as OC Nightflying out on the flarepath of that cold grass airfield. I was very fortunate in being given the chance to learn something of the problems confronting the bomber crews before being sent off on my own. Many pilots were not given this chance, although almost all of them had been trained at Wellington Operational Training Units which I had been denied. The most fortunate aspect of this period for me was being crewed with Pilot Officer Ron Simich, a New Zealander. He was an extremely competent bomber pilot, calm but determined, patient and knowledgeable with a unique capacity for imparting that knowledge. I learned more from him than from any other bomber source.'

By February 1941, when the long spell of bad weather lifted, Bomber Command had a dramatic new weapon in the shape of the Short Stirling. This was the first of the new generation of heavy bombers that had been ordered before the war, but only now were entering service. Powered by four engines and protected by eight machine guns mounted in three powered turrets, the Stirling promised to be a powerful striking weapon. However, it soon became clear that it was unable to operate much above 17,000 feet, which made it unpopular with crews. For the time being, however, it was the best that Bomber Command had. For the men of Norfolk, the matter was largely academic. They kept to their Blenheims and Wellingtons for more than another year.

Nor were the sorties undertaken from Norfolk going to alter much. The Blenheims continued to attack shipping and coastal targets, while the Wellingtons penetrated into Germany. One change that did come in March 1941 was the order to the Blenheim squadrons that they could attack anything that they saw, not just their designated targets. The new freedom was soon put to use by aircraft of No 82 Squadron. As they raced along the north German coast, the crews spotted a military parade taking place, which was promptly bombed.

The crew of a No 82 Squadron Blenheim flying out of Watton discovered the downside to such opportunistic attacks when on 31 March they dived down to attack an oil tanker off Le Havre. Beside the tanker was a small ship, loaded down with flak guns. Roaring in at a height of just 200 feet there was little that the pilot, Sergeant Robert Smith, could do to avoid the ack ack fire that came up at him. His starboard engine was smashed, and shrapnel riddled the aircraft. Smith and his crew had the satisfaction of seeing the tanker on fire as they left, but it was only owing to much luck and skill that the aircraft got home safely. The flak ships, as they became known, became increasingly common and dangerous as the months passed.

But it was not just the defences in and over enemy territory that could pose a threat. A new and dangerous development was discovered by a No 115 Squadron Wellington on the night of 10 February 1941. Sergeant Harold Rogers, the pilot, had been unable to bomb his main target due to heavy cloud cover so he was returning to base with a full bomb load. The weather cleared over Holland, so Rogers decided to use his weapons on a Luftwaffe base and made a successful attack. Not only were the bombs unloaded, but the gunners sprayed bullets around liberally in the hope of causing damage.

As Sergeant Rogers was approaching Marham, trouble struck in the shape of a Messerschmitt Bf 110 nightfighter. The German had been circling above Norfolk waiting for a returning bomber and he had spotted Rogers' aircraft. The British crew had their eyes on the ground and their thoughts on breakfast and bed when a hail of bullets and cannon shells tore though the bomber. The rear gunner was wounded, the port engine knocked out and the petrol tanks ruptured, spraying burning fuel over the port wing and along the fuselage. The aircraft was too low for the crew to bale out, so Rogers had to wrestle with the damaged controls to put his bomber down into a belly landing on the grass alongside the runway. As the Wellington skidded to a stop, Rogers and his crew leapt out, then returned to the blazing aircraft to drag the wounded gunner to safety. Orders soon went out to all bomber units to beware of German nightfighters operating over Britain.

Nevertheless, the Germans still took victims. On 11 May a Wellington was taking off on a sortie from Feltwell when it was attacked. Sergeant Joe Lawson, the navigator, recalled:

'Our rear gunner Sergeant Gannaway, from Hawke's Bay, New Zealand was killed by a Ju 88. Our aircraft was attacked from dead astern and the fighter must have seen us against the lighter sky. An armour-piercing 20 mm cannon shell went right through him. Tony Saunders, the second pilot, and myself went back to pull him out of the rear turret. We gave him morphine to deaden the pain and then tried to operate the turret but it was U/S [unserviceable]. We aborted the mission and returned to Feltwell. Gannaway didn't realise how badly injured he was and died shortly after we landed. He was buried in Feltwell cemetery and the funeral took the usual format – a slow march to the cemetery and after the burial the band striking up 'Colonel Bogie' as we marched away.'

On 1 May one of the most famous close escapes enjoyed by any Bomber Command aircraft was experienced by a crew of No 105 Squadron. Three Blenheims were sent out to launch an attack just after dawn on the oil refinery at Rotterdam. They roared in off the sea at very low level and got separated over the target area. The aircraft piloted by Flight Lieutenant George Goode left the attack scene, but was unlucky enough to be spotted

Sergeant Peter Gannaway, killed by one of the earliest appearances of the Ju 88 nightfighter. (www.feltwell.org)

by six Messerschmitt Bf 109s. The Luftwaffe launched a determined 20 minute attack. In the course of the fighting Goode was shot through the arm while his navigator, Pilot Officer Sam Hogan, had an ankle smashed and the gunner was wounded in the right hand.

Not only were the crew injured, but the Blenheim had been badly shot up. Moments after the Germans gave up the attack the port engine seized and the propeller fell off. Flight Lieutenant Goode tried desperately to gain height on his remaining engine, dragging the nose of the aircraft up although the tail controls were shot to pieces. After several minutes of tense drama the coast of England came within sight – at which point the starboard propeller suddenly fell off. The battered Blenheim was now without any propellers at all. The gunner, Sergeant Geoffrey Rowland, spotted a large ploughed field, and Goode put the Blenheim down without any undercarriage either.

Sergeant Rowland walked to a nearby farmhouse and phoned squadron base at Swanton Morley. An hour later the local ARP turned up in a car to take the wounded men to hospital. The crew soon became the focus of press attention. The story of the aircraft that came home with no propellers was splashed over the national press and the three men were, briefly, celebrities. All three were decorated with the DFM or DFC.

By the summer of 1941 Luftwaffe night defences were becoming increasingly effective. The key to their success was the system of 'boxes' known as *himmelbett*, or sky-beds. Each box covered several square miles of sky and was both patrolled by a nightfighter and swept regularly by ground-based radar. When the radar picked up a British bomber, the location of the aircraft was telephoned to searchlight batteries, which vectored in to find and illuminate the bomber. The nightfighter would then swoop in to try to shoot it down. The skies over Germany were becoming increasingly dangerous for British aircrew.

Officers of No 18 Squadron, with some female company, in the officers' mess at Little Massingham during that squadron's stay at the base in 1941. (Massingham MHSSLRAFMM)

Sergeant 'Chappie' Chapman of No 75 Squadron recalled a dramatic encounter with a nightfighter:

'We did Hamburg on three out of four consecutive nights in June 1941. On one of the trips we were gaining height as we headed out towards the coast near the Wash, which was our turning point for the track up the Frisian Islands. Minutes after we had crossed the coast my rear gunner, Jock, called me up over the intercom and told me that a fighter had latched on to us on the port quarter. A few cannon shells whistled past us so I put the aircraft into a very steep dive in an attempt to make him break off the attack. I soon noticed that the air speed indicator was registering off the scale as the fully loaded Wimpy [the slang name for the Wellington] gained momentum. I called up the crew and told them to yell as loud as they could when I started to pull out to stop them blacking out. I managed to pull out of the dive all right but I found that I could only fly the aircraft with the trim tabs set fully back. The aircraft flew like this okay so we did our raid and made it back to Feltwell. The next day I told our groundcrew 'Chiefy' what I had done. He asked me what speed I might have been doing, so I said maybe around 500 mph. Later on Chiefy jigged up the aircraft and found that I had bent both wing tips back by about 6 inches. That must have taken a lot of force but the Wimpy had handled it all right. They really were tough old kites.'

Another close escape was enjoyed by a No 75 Squadron crew on the way back from a raid on Hanover on 12 August. The Wellington was flown by Pilot Officer Hughie Roberts, and the raid was to be the last of the crew's first tour. On the return trip the aircraft was attacked over the Zuider Zee. Sergeant Paul Faguy, the Canadian rear gunner, opened up on the attacking Messerschmitt Bf 110 as bullets struck all around him. He later said: 'I felt a warm stickiness spreading from the top of my battle dress, and running down my leg. Seconds seemed like hours as I checked to see how badly I was wounded. Shock turned into heart-felt relief, as suddenly I realised that a cannon shell had pierced my coffee flask and that it was only warm coffee running down my uniform!' Meanwhile, the Wellington had sustained quite serious damage. The hydraulic system was badly knocked about and some fuel had been lost.

They were soon on the approach for Feltwell, seven hours after they had taken off, but due to the damage they were diverted to the emergency landing strip at Newmarket Heath. Suddenly, both of the aircraft's engines cut, the petrol had completely run out. At just under 1,000 feet Pilot Officer Roberts sounded the alarm and gave the order to bale out! Sergeant Faguy

The Wellington of Pilot Officer Hughie Roberts after it came to rest in a wood near RAF Feltwell. Amazingly the aircraft was repaired and returned to operations. (www.feltwell.org)

traversed the rear turret and pushed himself out backwards through the rear doors. The rest of the crew donned their parachutes, opened the emergency hatches and left the aircraft. Waiting for the crew to bale out, Roberts had left it too late. The aircraft was, by this time, too low for him to make good his escape. He remained in his seat, in control of a dead aircraft, pointed towards the Forestry Commission plantations between Weeting and Santon Downham.

The aircraft was suddenly very quiet, just the noise of the air hissing over the wings. With the loss of hydraulic pressure, the bomb bay doors gradually opened. In the distance, Pilot Officer Roberts could just make out a track between the trees. He held the aircraft off as long as he could, and then let it drop down onto a plantation of young firs. The trees rushed in through the open bomb bay doors and burst through into the inside of the aircraft. Suddenly, the aircraft was stationary, it had stopped level and straight! Switches off, Roberts left the aircraft without further delay. He walked along the forest track, which he had spotted earlier, for about 100 yards, when he ran into an Army patrol.

This Army patrol had orders to arrest anyone found within their area without permission. There followed what may be called an enlivened discussion. Roberts was very concerned about the fate of his crew and refused to be arrested until the patrol set out to look for them. He was then marched off under arrest to the Ram Hotel, Brandon, where the bar was open. This is how it came to pass, half an hour after one of the more exciting episodes of his life, that Pilot Officer Hughie Roberts (Australian) came to be drinking beer in the bar of the Ram Hotel. The rest of the crew were found scattered through the forest and likewise brought to the pub.

The grave of Sergeant Sydney Rishworth, pilot of the ill-fated Wellington that crashed at RAF Feltwell on 15 July 1941. (Shaun Smith)

The Wellington was deemed to be repairable and it was taken back to Vickers and rebuilt. It was eventually shot down over Germany. On that occasion, none of the airmen on board managed to escape.

Less fortunate was the crew of another Wellington that flew out of Feltwell on the 15 July 1941. Piloted by Sergeant Sydney Rishworth the bomber had as its target the railway marshalling yards at Duisburg. Over the target the Wellington was caught by searchlights and hit by flak. The port engine was knocked out, but Rishworth decided to make the attempt to return home to Feltwell on his remaining starboard engine.

As Sergeant Rishworth made his final approach the remaining engine

Sergeant Hugh Wright photographed in June 1941 when he was aged 21. One month later Wright was killed in the crash of which the only survivor was Sergeant Harry Lawson. He had been flying as wireless operator and is buried at Cadder Cemetery, Lanarkshire. (www.feltwell.org)

suddenly lost power, causing the bomber to dip earthwards. The aircraft clipped the top of a line of trees, burst into flames and dived into the road just west of the airfield. Emergency teams raced to the crash site and at considerable risk to themselves began trying to break into the burning bomber to rescue the crew.

Rear gunner Sergeant Harry Lawson was engulfed in flames. He could see burning perspex dripping on him and he found it fascinating to watch! He thought that his end had come. There was no way that he could know what was happening to his fellow crew members, so he said a prayer for them to be saved. This was not to be, but he was extremely fortunate that he was rescued from the plane – especially as this was the last flight of his first tour of duty.

Sergeant Lawson was hurriedly transferred to Ely Hospital where his injuries were so severe that a vicar was called to give him the last rites. Amazingly, Lawson survived and after much painful physiotherapy – then a new science – he returned to duty for a second tour. While he was convalescing, Lawson was several times wheeled out on a hospital trolley to see the sights of Ely by less badly injured air crew.

Another survivor of these desperate months was Squadron Leader William John Edrich, who is probably better known as the cricketer Bill Edrich. Edrich had already made his mark as a cricketer before the war began – he had faced India for Norfolk while still a schoolboy in Norwich and, in 1938, was part of the England team that visited Australia. The following year he again played for England, this time against South Africa, making an impressive 240 in the final Test.

As an officer in the RAF Volunteer Reserve, Edrich was called up as soon as war broke out. He served his first tour as a pilot officer in No 107 Squadron flying out of Great Massingham. He never let his cricket slide, however, and was famous for slipping away, whenever he could get permission, to play as a guest for one team or another. His fellow pilots wondered how he had the energy.

By 1941 Edrich had been promoted and transferred to No 21 Squadron flying out of Watton. There he picked up skills in a new sport – quoits – which was played regularly by aircrew on the base. He also led the famous Knapsack Raid, for which he was awarded a DFC. On 12th August, Edrich led his squadron, and others, to attack two large power stations at Cologne. The Blenheims had to fly 250 miles across enemy territory at a height of just 100 feet, then climb to 500 feet to deliver their attacks. The raid went like clockwork and both power stations were left as blazing ruins by the bombers.

Soon after this raid Edrich completed his second tour and was given a staff job for the rest of the war. His postwar career as a cricketer was to become the stuff of legend, but Edrich never forgot his time with the RAF in his native Norfolk and often stated that, unlike so many of his comrades, he had survived by sheer luck and was determined to live life to the full.

It was in August 1941 that the famous Butt Report was produced. This was kept top secret at the time, and with good reason. The report studied photographs of damage caused by raids in June and July 1941 in great detail – special photographic sorties being flown to get accurate data for the first time. It was found that only 25% of crews attacking targets in Germany got to within five miles of their aiming point. Over well defended targets, such as the Ruhr factories, the ratio fell to a depressing 10%. Hardly any bombs

A 500 lb blast bomb is hoisted on to a bomb trolley before being loaded onto a Wellington of No 115 Squadron in 1941. These pre-war bombs were filled with amatol, which proved to be ineffective against heavy buildings. Later bombs were filled with TNT.

actually hit the factory or oil plant at which they were supposedly aimed. Navigation was the main problem, though bomb-aiming was also identified as an issue.

Air Chief Marshal Peirse was still trying to digest the full import of the Butt Report when he had the chance to show what Bomber Command could do. On 7 November, he took advantage of a new moon and a lack of demand for operations by the Navy to launch a major strategic bombing raid, larger than anything that had taken place before. The bulk of the force was sent to Berlin, with smaller forces heading for Mannheim or the Ruhr. In all, 392 heavy bombers were sent out. At the last moment the commander of No 5 Group in Lincolnshire diverted his bombers, originally scheduled to attack Berlin, to Cologne instead after he became concerned by forecasts of deteriorating weather.

The night proved to be a disaster for Bomber Command. A total of 37 bombers were lost. Several went down to the increasingly effective German defences, but others fell victim to icing-up or ran out of fuel due to the strong headwinds they met on the way home. Several aircraft that returned safely did so on near empty tanks. Only the No 5 Group bombers got back without loss. Of those sent to Berlin a terrible 13% of aircraft were lost.

Prime Minister Winston Churchill immediately stepped in to impose a direct order. Large scale raids to targets deep inside Germany were banned. As Churchill pointed out, new long-range bombers were in production, as well as improved night navigation equipment. These would be entering service in the spring and, until then, the bombers must be sent to targets that were closer to home.

On 4 January 1942 Air Marshal Sir Charles Portal, as Chief of the Air Staff, showed Prime Minister Churchill a final report on the disastrous raid against Berlin that had taken place on 7 November. It proved beyond doubt that Air Chief Marshal Peirse had known about the forecast bad weather, but had ordered the raid to go ahead anyway. Churchill was appalled that so many men had been killed for so little effect when the whole operation had been avoidable. Peirse was removed from his post immediately.

Bomber Command was about to get a new commander. But before he makes an appearance, there were two outstanding events in 1941 that deserve to be related in their own right – the Brest raid and, in separate actions, the award of the Victoria Cross to two airmen flying from Norfolk airfields.

Bristol Blenheim IV

Type:	Medium bomber
Engines:	2 x 920 hp Bristol Mercury XV
Wingspan:	56 ft 4 in
Length:	42 ft 7 in
Height:	9 ft 10 in
Weight:	Empty 9,790 lb Loaded 13,500 lb
Armament:	2 (later 3) x 0.303 in machine guns in wing and dorsal turret
Bomb-load:	1,320 lb of bombs
Max speed:	266 mph
Ceiling:	24,600 ft
Range:	1,400 miles
Production:	3,922

The Blenheim IV was a development of the Blenheim, which had entered service with the RAF in 1937. As the Mk IV entered service in 1939, the old Mk I aircraft were stripped of their bombs to make way for additional guns and the war's first airborne radar set. The most noticeable external difference was the long glazed nose of the Mk IV, though the key changes were internal. It was designed largely to support the army by striking at tactical targets close behind enemy lines, but this role was abandoned once France fell in June 1940. The Blenheim IV thereafter proved to be a highly effective fast strike bomber in the early war years, though its relatively limited range meant that it could be used only against coastal or marine targets. By 1942 the Blenheim IV was proving to be increasingly vulnerable to German fighters, so it was transferred to second line duties in India and other theatres. By 1942 both the Mk I and Mk IV had been largely replaced in combat by other models.

Chapter 3

The Brest Raid

On 24 July 1941 there took place one of the most daring raids of the war. Certainly it earned Bomber Command more medals than any other single action. A total of five Distinguished Service Orders (DSO), 26 Distinguished Flying Crosses (DFC) and 20 Distinguished Flying Medals (DFM) were awarded for an action that lasted less than an hour.

At this stage in the war, Atlantic convoys were being hit often and severely by German U-boats. Even worse, from the Royal Navy's point of view, was the threat posed by Germany's big surface warships. Any one of these ships was so powerful that it could sink an entire convoy in less than half an hour. The mere fact that one was at sea was enough to cancel all convoys in the area.

In June 1941 reconnaissance aircraft photographed three warships – *Scharnhorst*, *Gneisenau* and *Prinz Eugen* – in the occupied French port of Brest. At the request of the Navy, Bomber Command made an effort to bomb the ships at night. Pilot Officer Arthur Ashworth of No 75 Squadron later said of this mission:

'On the 18th of June we took off for another attack on Brest, this time trying to hit the *Scharnhorst*. We spent a considerable time over the target area and finally established, by the light of one of our flares, that the *Scharnhorst* was not berthed where we had been briefed to find her. However, there was another large ship in the harbour and this we attacked.

A reconnaisance photo taken in preparation for the Brest raid.
Key: (1) Scharnhorst *and* Gneisenau *docked at Brest. The ships are sewn to the quay*
by camouflage netting while stagings have been built on the hull to disguise their
shape; (2) Camouflaged buildings; (3) Anti-torpedo nets; (4) Oil tanks.

On the way home we got ourselves lost by misidentifying our landfall. As a consequence we flew through the balloon barrage at Bristol. It was just breaking daylight when this happened and there was quite a bit of anxiety in that aircraft until we were clear. My log book records only that we were lost and came through the balloon barrages, but for this particular flight I was awarded the DFC.'

Pilot Officer Ashworth was being modest. The contemporary account in the *London Gazette* reads:

'Although the target was obscured, Pilot Officer Ashworth flew over the area for a considerable time, finally dropping flares immediately both north and south of the target, which enabled him to see and attack his objective. He also aimed one bomb at an unidentified vessel of 10,000 tons which was observed to be entering the docks. Pilot Officer Ashworth made eight surveying runs, at times at an extremely low altitude and in the face of intense anti-aircraft fire. He displayed outstanding skill, courage and infinite care in his efforts to bomb accurately.'

On 22 July the *Scharnhorst* left Brest and it was feared that the other two were about to follow and join her on a massively destructive raid through the shipping lanes of the Atlantic. The Navy contacted Bomber Command to ask if an attack could be mounted within 48 hours. Air Chief Marshal Peirse agreed.

Because of the need for great accuracy when bombing German ships in a French port, it was decided to attack in daylight. The large force of Wellingtons and Hampdens was to fly at low level in the hope of avoiding detection, and would be escorted throughout by Spitfires operating from Cornwall and Devon. They were given a route that took them around Brittany, keeping out of sight of land and away from any known German shipping routes. In a further attempt to reduce losses on this potentially hazardous daylight mission, a force of Blenheims, again with Spitfire escort, was detailed to attack Cherbourg to create a diversion and lure German fighters away from Brest. So desperate was the need to disable the ships that Peirse even sent a small force of B-17 Flying Fortresses that he had on trial

A Boeing B-17 Flying Fortress of No 90 Squadron takes off to participate in the Brest raid. The RAF had taken delivery of 20 Model C Fortresses earlier in 1941 on a trial basis. The large American bombers proved to be weak in defensive armament and rather clumsy at altitude. Later models, used mostly by the USAAF, had more than double the number of defensive machine guns, including a new rear gunner position and a chin gun mounting under the nose, with a redesigned tail to aid performance at altitude.

from America. These aircraft were to bomb from a height of over 30,000 feet in an effort to evade German defences.

As might have been expected, all these precautions managed to achieve only a moderate success. The Germans were as determined to defend their ships as the British were to attack them.

By the time No 115 Squadron came roaring in the German defences were thoroughly awake. A Messerschmitt Bf 109 quickly got on the tail of the Wellington in which Sergeant Albert Adderley was rear gunner. He was on his 43rd operational mission and had won a reputation for coolness under fire. He certainly lived up to it as he held his nerve even though the Luftwaffe guns shattered the perspex dome of his turret. Not until he was certain of his aim did Adderley let rip, watching with satisfaction as the German immediately flipped over and dived straight into the sea.

Meanwhile Sergeant John Cork, rear gunner in another No 115 Squadron Wellington, was in serious difficulties. An attacking Bf 109 had fired a burst of gunfire that smashed the turret perspex and ripped to shreds the hydraulics pipes, dousing the unfortunate Cork in fluids that stung his eyes and temporarily blinded him. As he fought to wipe his eyes clear, Cork heard his captain calling down the intercom that a second fighter was approaching from the port quarter. Unable to see, Cork loosed off a burst of fire in what he hoped was the right direction. It was. The Messerschmitt dived away with its wing clearly damaged.

If anything No 75 Squadron fared even worse. They came in at higher altitude, hoping that by this time the Luftwaffe fighters would all be down at low altitude and would not trouble with climbing to attack. Their hopes were dashed by a full squadron of Bf 109s that were circling even higher.

In the run in towards the *Gneisenau*, No 75 Squadron's designated target, the flak was astonishingly heavy. The lead aircraft was to be responsible for guiding in the others and for giving the signal to bomb. It was hit by flak which tore away a section of the aircraft floor just behind the spot where Observer Gwyn Martin was lying with his eye glued to the bombsight. With great coolness, Martin did not even look up. He sent his bombs whistling down to strike the dock just behind the battleship, with the rest of the formation's bombs straddling the ship.

One Luftwaffe fighter dived down even before the Wellingtons were clear of the German flak. It was engaged by Sergeant Herrold Corrin from his rear turret at a range of 300 yards and forced to change direction. Three of the Messerschmitts converged on the Wellington in which Sergeant Edward

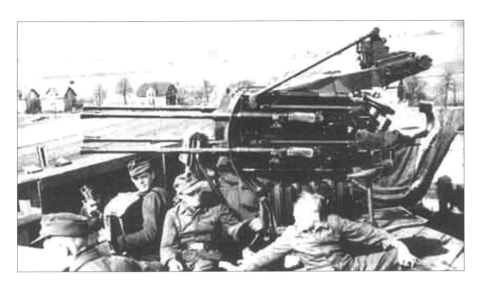

A German gun crew manning a light flak weapon. These light weapons could be horribly effective against bombers attacking at low level, as during the Brest raid.

Callander was rear gunner. Their concentrated fire put the front turret out of action, and badly shot up the cockpit area. Unperturbed, Callander returned fire, shooting down one enemy fighter and driving off the other two. The Luftwaffe returned, shot down the Wellington beside that of Callander and again positioned to attack. This time Callander let rip with a lengthy burst of over 600 rounds that he hosed around to such effect that the Germans left No 75 Squadron alone. This was just as well, for every single Wellington of the squadron was damaged to the extent that they had to be taken for repair.

Even away from the immediate vicinity of Brest the raiders were not safe. One of the B-17s of No 90 Squadron was attacked by seven Luftwaffe fighters while cruising at 32,000 feet. Perched in the mighty bomber's astrodome was Sergeant Norman Goldsmith. His task was to spot approaching enemy fighters, relaying their direction and speed to the pilot so that he could take evasive action and to the gunners so that they could shoot accurately.

The first attack by the Germans killed both beam gunners, seriously weakening the defensive fire available. In the next five minutes the rear gunner and upper gunner were both killed. Then Sergeant Goldsmith was shot through the leg. Nevertheless he stayed at his post in the astrodome, calmly keeping up a running commentary for the pilot on the movements of the enemy. With no defensive gunfire to worry about, the German fighters were able to close to point blank range. Still Goldsmith's instructions allowed the pilot to jink and turn so as to avoid the attacks. Not until the bomber was down to 8,000 feet and far out over the Channel did the Luftwaffe break off.

The battered Flying Fortress crashlanded on the first available airfield after reaching England and the aircraft caught fire. Even though his left leg was by now dangling useless, Sergeant Goldsmith managed to help the unwounded pilot drag the bodies of their dead comrades from the wreck.

The raid was judged to have been an operational success. The *Gneisenau* was hit, and the *Prinz Eugen* suffered several near misses. Both ships were out of action for some months. The missing *Scharnhorst* had been found at La Pallice and likewise damaged by bombs, so badly that she had to go into dry dock.

Chapter 4

The Two VCs

In one hectic week in July 1941 two airmen of Bomber Command in Norfolk were awarded the Victoria Cross, the highest award for gallantry in action. Both men came from the colonies, but otherwise were very different characters united only by their outstanding bravery in the face of the enemy.

Hughie Idwal Edwards had been born in Western Australia, the son of Welsh immigrants, on 1 August 1914. At the age of 20 he joined the army to serve in the local artillery, but in 1935 transferred to the Royal Australian Air Force (RAAF) before joining the RAF the following year. In 1937 he began his flying career as a pilot on Blenheim Mk I bombers with No 90 Squadron. He was, therefore, an experienced professional by the time he was appointed to command No 105 Squadron at Swanton Morley in May 1941.

Wing Commander Edwards had led his squadron on several sweeps across the North Sea hunting for German ships before, on 4 July, he was ordered to lead Operation Wreckage, an attack on the docks at Bremen. This would be his 36th operational flight and he was to have under his command not only No 105 Squadron, but also six Blenheims from No 107 Squadron. Edwards briefed his men to fly to Bremen in tight formation, but on arrival they were to form up into a line abreast, each aircraft some 400 feet apart from the others. He hoped in this way to ensure that each aircraft found a worthwhile target while keeping to a minimum the chance that two bombers would go for the same victim. The attack was to be quick and destructive, with the Blenheims wasting no time before racing back out to sea towards England.

The formation flew over the sea at around 100 feet to avoid German radar, roaring over the coast at Cuxhaven. As soon as they were over land the aircraft were spotted and the air defences of Bremen soon began to throw up flak and machine gun fire. Wing Commander Edwards led his aircraft through the outer ring of defences and negotiated a field of barrage balloons before giving the order for the formation to form up abreast.

By this time Wing Commander Edwards had his Blenheim down to just 50 feet and only narrowly avoided hitting a telephone wire strung between a pole and an office building. Seconds later he flew under an electricity power line before spotting a large factory. Turning slightly to get over the target, he dropped his bomb dead on target. His navigator, Pilot Officer Ramsay,

This photograph of the factory bombed by Edwards in the raid on Bremen was taken by Pilot Officer Ramsay.

Wing Commander Hughie Edwards VC (facing the camera) photographed after receiving the news that he had been awarded the Victoria Cross.

took a famous photograph looking back over the aircraft's tail showing the factory just before it was torn apart by the bombs.

Blenheims at this time were generally equipped with bombs that had an eleven-second fuse. This meant that they exploded eleven seconds after striking the target, giving the aircraft time to get clear of the blast wave. Unfortunately, the crews were very often unable to see whether or not their bombs had hit the target intended. The attempt to take photographs of the bomb blast was made so that they could later be studied by experts to determine what sort of wreckage was being thrown up and where the base of the blast was located.

Pilot Officer Ramsay took his photograph too early and by the time he had wound the camera on the factory was well out of sight. There was, however, little doubt that the target had been hit as the factory disintegrated in the blast with debris flying 700 feet into the air, well above the height of the aircraft that had dropped the bombs.

Wing Commander Edwards flew on at rooftop level right across Bremen and out to the other side of the city. By the time he left the outer defences his aircraft had been under fire for ten minutes and hit 20 times. The gunner, Sergeant Quinn, was wounded in the leg. This was the second time that Quinn had been wounded in action. The first occasion had been when he was gunner in a Fairey Battle of No 40 Squadron based at Betheniville in France. His pilot on that flight in May 1940, Flight Lieutenant Smeddle, had been leading an attack on the advancing German hordes in May 1940 when a cannon shell exploded beside the aircraft, tearing off the top of the fuselage and wounding Quinn, who had continued to fire his guns at the enemy and was awarded a DFM for the feat.

Most of the other Blenheims had also been hit. One aircraft from No 105 Squadron returned to Swanton Morley with its hydraulic system destroyed and was forced to crash land. A second landed safely, only for the crew to find a length of telephone cable trailing from the tail wheel. Others were not so lucky. Both Nos 105 and 107 Squadrons lost two bombers over the target. A third No 105 Blenheim was last seen with an engine on fire continuing its bombing run to hit its chosen target and then heading south as if seeking a place to land. It was not until many months later that the men of No 105 learned that the crew had died when the aircraft crashed.

For his leadership and calm bravery in action, Wing Commander Edwards was awarded the Victoria Cross. His gunner, Sergeant Quinn, got a bar to his DFM while other men on the sortie received DFCs and DFMs. Edwards went on to win the DSO for his role in a raid in December 1942 that destroyed an electronics factory in Eindhoven and finished the war as a Group Captain in Malaya. He retired from the RAF in 1963 with the rank of Air Commodore and was knighted in 1974. He died at home in Australia in 1982.

The second action that led to a Norfolk Bomber Command VC took place just three days later on 7 July. The recipient this time was a quiet schoolteacher from New Zealand named James Allen Ward. Ward had volunteered in July 1940, finally reaching No 75 Squadron at Feltwell as a pilot in June 1941 at the age of just 21.

It was on Sergeant Ward's seventh operation that he worked his way to a VC. He was second pilot to Squadron Leader R. Widdowson on a Wellington that was part of a force sent to bomb Munster. The raid was carried out by 41 aircraft, ten of them from No 75 Squadron, and went largely without incident. The return trip took Widdowson over the Zuider Zee at a height of 13,000 feet. Suddenly he saw an ominous twin-engined silhouette to his left. Recognising it as a Messerschmitt Bf 110 nightfighter, Widdowson turned

Flight Sergeant James Ward photographed outside the chapel in South Street, Hockwold. At this time he was billeted at the Rectory, Hockwold. The photograph is thought to have been taken by the Hockwold policeman of the time.

to starboard. It was a trap. Lurking beneath the Wellington was a second Bf 110 which now climbed up to rake the bomber from front to rear with a savage fusillade of cannon shells. The central area of the Wellington was riddled with holes, the hydraulics system punctured, the radio smashed and the starboard engine set on fire.

The rear gunner, Sergeant Allen Box, was wounded in the foot, but he forgot his wound almost immediately as the Messerschmitt climbed past him, exposing its own underbelly. He pumped 200 rounds into the German aircraft, seeing it fall earthwards with smoke pouring from one engine. He tried to report back to Widdowson, but the intercom had been destroyed in the attack. Box could see the flaming engine, but reasoned that so long as the aircraft was flying straight and level, the rest of the crew had not baled out. He too stayed at his post, scanning the skies for enemy planes although he had no idea what was going on in the rest of his own aircraft.

In fact, Squadron Leader Widdowson had decided to abandon the aircraft and ordered his crew to don their parachutes. Sergeant Ward, however, had other ideas. He tore a hole in the fabric side of the Wellington and tried to put out the engine fire with an extinguisher. The foam was blown away before it could have any effect. Ward then turned to the navigator, Sergeant Lawton, and said, 'I think I'll hop out to do this.' Widdowson refused to allow Ward to make the attempt, but agreed after he put on a parachute and tied the rope from the dinghy around his waist and got Lawton to hold the other end.

Thus equipped, Sergeant Ward removed the cover from the astrodome and crawled out through the hole. He used his flying boots to kick holes in the fabric, and so get a grip on the metal struts that made up the geodetic frame of the Wellington. Slowly he worked his way down the side of the fuselage onto the wing. The main fear was that the fire would set alight the fabric covering the wing. With this gone the wing would generate no lift and the Wellington would crash. Ward intended to stuff a heavy canvas engine cover into the fire and so douse the flames, or at least stop them reaching the vulnerable fabric.

Sergeant Ward slowly inched his way out along the wing until he was next to the flaming engine. Then he used his right arm to shove the canvas sheet into the hole and smother the flames. As soon as he let go, the slipstream tugged the cover free, so he pushed it back. He held it there for several minutes until his left arm could no longer stand the strain of supporting him against the slipstream. Ward let go again, and the canvas cover was whipped away. The fire was not out, but was now merely a wisp of flame. Hoping for the best, he inched back towards the fuselage.

It was only with a great deal of pulling from Sergeant Lawton that the exhausted Ward managed to get back into the aircraft. Having reported back to Squadron Leader Widdowson, he collapsed in a heap. Widdowson turned the aircraft out over the North Sea, heading for the emergency landing strip near Newmarket.

The battered Wellington reached Newmarket just as dawn was breaking. With no brakes due to the smashed hydraulics system, the Wellington careered across the grass airfield and piled up into the boundary hedge. Only then did the rear gunner, Sergeant Box, clamber out of his turret to ask his colleagues what had been going on. He was soon whisked off to hospital while the rest of the crew travelled back to Feltwell by lorry. Sergeant Box was awarded a DFM for his coolness, while Squadron Leader Widdowson was awarded a DFC. Sergeant Ward, of course, was awarded a Victoria Cross.

Sergeant 'Chappie' Chapman, who shared a room with Ward at Feltwell, explains what happened after the epic flight:

'After Jimmy was awarded the VC he was taken off operations for three weeks so that he could go to Buckingham Palace to collect his medal. After this we would go to the sergeants' mess at Feltwell and as soon as Jimmy walked in everyone would stand up and salute. Whenever this happened Jimmy would do a quick 180 degrees and walk out, he was very shy about the whole thing. But this meant that we were both living on sandwiches, so I had a word with the lads and they packed it in. At the end of the three weeks Jimmy became captain of his own aircraft; on his first trip as captain they had some trouble and landed away from Feltwell. On 15th September, when he was on his second trip, (Hamburg), he was shot down over the target and killed.'

On his return from collecting his VC at Buckingham Palace, James Ward was met at the railway station by aircrew and carried shoulder high back to base.

Chapter 5

A New Commander

When **Air Chief Marshal Sir Richard Peirse** was dismissed as head of Bomber Command, neither Portal nor Churchill had decided who would take his place. As a temporary measure the popular commander of No 3 Group, Air Vice Marshal Jack Baldwin, was moved to assume control. Baldwin was told not to introduce any major changes, so he continued with the pattern of raids already established. So far as Norfolk was concerned, this meant attacking coastal targets with Blenheim squadrons and pushing deeper into Germany with Wellingtons.

There was, however, one major strategic change that occurred during Baldwin's time in command. The government approved a new operational directive to govern Bomber Command's actions. It reached Baldwin on 14 February 1942 and ordered him to direct the main weight of Bomber Command for the next six months into what were known as Area Bombing raids on major German industrial cities.

The new directive had grown out of the Butt Report of the previous year. It was recognised that bomber crews, flying at night, simply could not identify individual factories or installations. Indeed, some crews did well if they identified the right town. In effect Bomber Command was being told to abandon any attempt to find and destroy individual targets at night – although day bombers operating along the enemy coast would still be directed at such targets. Instead Area Bombing involved identifying areas

The statue of Air Chief Marshal Sir Arthur Harris that stands in London outside St Clement Danes, the home church of the RAF. The erection of the statue as a memorial to the men of Bomber Command was not undertaken until the 1990s and even then proved to be controversial due to the ruthless determination with which Harris pursued the bombing campaign against Germany.

63

that were large enough so that the crews could be relied upon to find them and that contained enough economic or transportation targets to ensure that some at least would be hit by bombers striking the area. Since the majority of factories and rail junctions tend to lie in towns and cities, the Area Bombing directive effectively pointed Bomber Command at pounding industrial cities. Even if the precise targets themselves were missed, the destruction of nearby buildings would block roads and rail links, effectively making the factories unproductive for some days. Moreover, the destruction of housing near the factories would mean that the workers had nowhere to live, further disrupting war production.

The fact that such cities were packed with civilians could no longer be a restraining factor for the RAF. Britain and Germany were engaged in a total war. The civilians were workers in factories producing guns, aircraft and munitions of all kinds. In any case, as it was seen at the time, the Germans had started it with their indiscriminate bombing of Warsaw, Coventry, London and a dozen other cities. For the rest of the war, Bomber Command would have as its main priority the destruction of Germany's ability to equip, feed and maintain its armed forces.

What the Chief of the Air Staff, Sir Charles Portal, needed was a commander willing and able to put this new strategy into destructive effect. On 22 February 1942 he found his man in the shape of Air Chief Marshal Sir Arthur Harris – soon to be better known as 'Bomber Harris'.

Harris had been born in Gloucestershire in 1892, but moved to Rhodesia as a teenager. He spent the early months of the Great War fighting against German colonial troops in East Africa before joining the Royal Flying Corps and moving to France. He later flew fighters protecting London from the Zeppelin menace. After the war he stayed on in what was to become the Royal Air Force and when the Second World War broke out was commanding No 5 Group of Bomber Command. In 1940 he moved to London to become Deputy Head of the Air Staff and then went to Washington to act as a liaison officer to the American government. It was from this post that he was recalled to take control of Bomber Command.

Harris was famously competent and frighteningly efficient, demanding nothing less than excellence from his subordinates. He was neither jovial nor overtly friendly. He did not believe in visiting squadrons to give pep talks or improve morale. Nor did he believe in handing out praise, medals or compliments. So far as Harris was concerned he was there to do a job to the best of his abilities and so was everybody else. So long as he and his men achieved that he was satisfied. Defaulters were dispensed with swiftly, almost brutally, but those who worked hard were kept on and promoted. His men adored him.

At the time Harris took command some important changes to Bomber Command equipment were taking place. Most of these related to aircraft, but some were concentrated on navigation – long a serious problem with night bombing.

The aircraft arriving for service with Bomber Command came in a variety of shapes and sizes. The new heavy bombers – the Lancaster and the Halifax – would gradually replace the older twin-engine night bombers. At first the new models were allocated elsewhere, the squadrons in Norfolk continuing to use their trusty Wellingtons for some months to come.

An armourer fuses up a 4,000 lb 'cookie' bomb. The 'cookie' was introduced in 1941 after it was found that the pre-war 2,000 lb Mk IV bomb was largely ineffective against anything but the flimsiest buildings.

A Boston, probably of No 88 Squadron flying from RAF Oulton in spring 1943. By this date the later 'DB-7B' model of Boston with a greater range and larger bomb-load was in service. (Massingham MHSSLRAFMM)

More immediately, the aging Blenheims began to be replaced by Bostons and Venturas. Both these aircraft were bought in from the USA under the Lend-Lease scheme that allowed Britain to acquire weapons on credit – the final bill not being due to be paid until 2006. The first to arrive was the Douglas DB-7 Boston, which began arriving in July 1940. These had actually been ordered by France in August 1939 but when France surrendered, the aircraft were taken over by the RAF. The Boston could fly 90 mph faster than the Blenheim and carry twice the bomb-load, making it a much more effective raider. By the middle of 1942 the RAF had around 1,000 Bostons in service.

The Lockheed PV-1 Ventura arrived later, the first aircraft reaching Britain in July 1942. In theory its performance was comparable to that of the Boston, but in combat crews found it clumsy and it took higher casualties than did the Douglas aircraft. Where the Ventura did have the edge was on range for it could fly 1,660 miles, about twice as far as the Boston. By the end of 1943 the Ventura was mostly being used as a long range naval patrol bomber in the war against the U-boats.

Also in the spring of 1942, the navigational aid Gee was being fitted to operational bombers for the first time. The system relied on the aircraft fitted with Gee picking up three radio signals transmitted from stations in Britain located 200 miles apart. By triangulation the aircraft could fix its position to within a few hundred yards when up to 400 miles or so from base. This was not good enough to locate individual targets in bad weather, but did at least allow pilots to be confident that they were over the right town.

That navigational problems were not just a matter of hitting the right target, but could mean life or death to the crew, was shown by a peculiar event at Feltwell on the night of 25 February 1942. In the early hours of

The Bostons of No 107 Squadron are lined up for inspection at Great Massingham soon after their arrival in March 1942. (Massingham MHSSLRAFMM)

The electricians who kept the more sophisticated radio and navigational equipment working on the aircraft flying out of Great Massingham in the autumn of 1942. Those who can be identified are: Front: LAC Alf Woods. Seated left to right:

Cpl Barry Foulger, Cpl Paddy ?, F/Sgt Burgess, Cpl Dulgarh; Standing left to right: LAC Jock Duncan, six unknowns, LAC Johnny Eberle, LAC Ted May. (Massingham MHSSLRAFMM)

the morning a farmer was getting up to attend to his livestock when he heard a scuffling noise outside. Dousing his light to comply with blackout regulations, the man slipped into his yard. His eyes were not yet accustomed to the dark, but he did manage to spot a furtive figure wheeling his bike away. The farmer at once ran after the would-be thief, who turned to deliver a stinging punch before he was wrestled to the ground. The bike thief was eventually overpowered and turned out to be an RAF sergeant dressed in full flying kit.

Despite the farmer's repeated questions, the sergeant refused to say a word. Not until an officer was brought from RAF Feltwell did the man, who turned out to be Sergeant Spalding of No 15 Squadron, say anything. Up until that moment he had been convinced that he was in Germany and that the farmer's questions in English had been a ruse to get him to talk.

Sergeant Spalding's aircraft, a Stirling, had been on a raid to Sylt when it was hit by flak. All radio and navigational equipment was destroyed. After flying for some time in what he hoped was the right direction the pilot, Squadron Leader Wilson, saw a stretch of water in front of him. Reasoning this must be the North Sea, Wilson checked his instruments. He had barely enough fuel to cross to England. Wilson gave each member of the crew the choice of baling out to be captured, or risk starting on a crossing that they might not finish. And with no way of calling up the Navy to rescue them, the crew would be most unlikely to survive if they did ditch in the sea. Spalding opted to bale out, the rest stayed with the aircraft.

Sergeant Spalding had floated to earth in what he thought was northern Germany. He guessed his best chance would be to head west to reach Holland and then try to find a friendly face to help him contact the resistance. Finding what he took to be a German bike at a German farm, Spalding had tried to steal it with the results already seen.

Meanwhile, Squadron Leader Wilson had run out of fuel sooner than he expected. He ordered the crew to get the life raft ready and prepare to land on water. The heavy bomber came down without undercarriage and, after some buffeting, slid to a stop. The disorientated crew threw out the raft and jumped after it, only find themselves in a broad grassy field. They were still debating what to do when the Home Guard arrived.

Spalding, Wilson and the others were lucky. So were the crew of an unknown bomber who ditched in the North Sea on the night of 26 June. They came down without being able to radio their location back to base and must have thought themselves doomed to a watery grave as they were over a hundred miles east of Norfolk. Amazingly the tiny raft was spotted by Sergeant John Jenkins, a gunner on a No 115 Squadron Wellington returning from a raid. The bomber came down to circle the raft, constantly sending out a radio signal so that a naval rescue boat could home in and save the men.

Many other bomber crews ditched in the North Sea and did not make it. So greatly did some crews fear ditching that they went to great lengths to avoid it. On 3 June No 115 Squadron had been sent to bomb Bremen. One Wellington was badly damaged on the way out and turned for home before reaching the target. Once over the North Sea the pilot realised that he had lost all the fuel in the starboard wing tanks. The fuel pump from the emergency tank would not work, so the crew members took it in turns to operate the stiff manual pump to move fuel from the nascelle to the starboard engine and so get home safely.

The Honourable William Jordan, High Commissioner for New Zealand, pays an official visit to No 75 Squadron in summer 1942. The vast majority of personnel in this squadron were New Zealanders. (www.feltwell.org)

Meanwhile, the bombing raids carried on much as before. In April No 75 Squadron was sent to attack Cologne. In line with the new Area Bombing directive, the crews were not given specific factories to try to find, but were directed to an area of the city centre where several worthwhile targets were known to be.

Returning from the raid, the Wellington piloted by Flight Sergeant Ivor McLachlan was suddenly attacked by a Luftwaffe nightfighter. The concentrated spray of machine gun bullets killed the second pilot and badly wounded the tail gunner. The aircraft suffered total hydraulics failure, causing the undercarriage and bomb doors to fall open, while the flaps dropped. As the bomber fell into a crazily spinning dive, both gun turrets jammed and the radio equipment failed completely. It was no doubt in the belief that the bomber was doomed that the German broke off his attack.

In fact Flight Sergeant McLachlan, who was on his 19th operation, got the

The Wellington was famously robust and able to withstand terrible punishment. This aircraft was hit by flak over Germany and set on fire. The crew extinguished the flames and flew the bomber home despite the extensive damage.

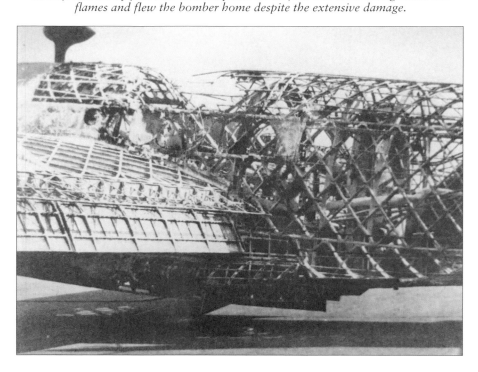

Wellington under control. He nursed the bomber back to Feltwell, putting it down in a belly landing on the grass. Not content with this, he led his unwounded front gunner to the rear of the aircraft to pull the wounded tail gunner free of the wreckage. 'This NCO has set an example of great fortitude,' noted the station commander, 'by crash-landing his aircraft to the left of the flare path where he knew he would cause no obstruction to other aircraft landing.'

On the same raid, the aircraft flown by Pilot Officer Eric Jarman, an Australian, was hit over Cologne by an ack ack shell that wounded the front gunner, navigator and wireless operator. Despite the damage, Jarman continued his run to bomb on target before turning for England.

As the damaged Wellington headed north, the second pilot discovered that one bomb had not dropped. Before anything could be done, the bomber was attacked by a Luftwaffe fighter which flashed past with all guns blazing. The tail gunner was killed outright and the second pilot wounded. This left Pilot Officer Jarman as the only unwounded crew member. More seriously, the undercarriage was damaged beyond use. Jarman realised that his crew were too wounded to bale out, but with a hung-up bomb he could not crash-land.

For more than 45 minutes the less wounded crew members wrestled to free the fatal bomb, while Pilot Officer Jarman sought to keep the stricken bomber on course. Finally, as the bomber crossed the sea the bomb was dropped. Jarman then headed for the nearest emergency landing air strip, and put his bomber down in a belly landing on the grass with such skill that no further injuries were sustained.

Not all pilots had given up on more precise accuracy. Pilot Officer Douglas Rohde of No 115 Squadron at Marham was one who did not like to waste bombs. He gave his crew a real fright in July when they were attacking Saarbrucken. Solid cloud covered the target, so Rohde simply dived straight down through it. He came out below the bottom of the cloud at under 3,000 feet, dragging the nose of his bomber up before they hit the ground and just in time to bomb a railway before climbing back up into the cloud.

While the Wellingtons probed into Germany, the Blenheims, Bostons and Venturas continued to harry targets close to the coast. Eindhoven airfield, a noted Luftwaffe base, was attacked by No 114 Squadron out of West Raynham. On the outward journey the gunner in the aircraft flown by Pilot Officer Molesworth reported that his turret was out of action. Rather than turn back, he flew on to bomb Eindhoven successfully from 2,000 feet.

Wing Commander Richard England (in peaked cap), commander of No 114 Squadron, poses with WO Baker, Sergeant Kendall and Sergeant Lennett in front of his Blenheim at West Raynham in 1942.

Unfortunately Pilot Officer Molesworth's aircraft was promptly attacked by a German nightfighter. The first the British crew knew of the attack was when the instrument panel exploded in a shower of glass and metal fragments as machine gun bullets reduced it to pieces and a huge hole was torn in the cockpit floor by a cannon shell. Nobody was injured, but the aircraft was barely under control. While Molesworth struggled to keep the Blenheim on course, his observer, Pilot Officer Edmund Denny, crawled back through the shattered fuselage to check on the gunner who was by now trapped in his jammed turret.

Pilot Officer Molesworth got the aircraft to England and crash-landed into a field. Both engines promptly burst into flames. Although the fire was spreading rapidly to the fuselage, both he and Pilot Officer Denny scrambled along the fuselage to smash open the turret and extricate their gunner. All three men were burned, but survived.

With his new aircraft and navigational equipment, Air Chief Marshal Harris decided to try a new idea. He had become convinced that some of Bomber Command's problems arose from the fact that most bombers found their own way to a target. This meant that the attacking force arrived over the target spread out in both time and space. This, Harris thought, made them both poor at aiming and vulnerable to defences. Harris believed that if a large force arrived all at once both problems could be solved. He decided to try out his ideas in dramatic fashion: He would send 1,000 bombers to attack Hamburg in less than an hour.

Many days of careful planning went into what was dubbed Operation Millennium. A concept known as 'streaming' was developed. This put all the aircraft into one or more streams with all the bombers flying in the same direction at a similar height and speed. In theory each aircraft had its own exact place in the mass of bombers, but in practice this was difficult to maintain and pilots had to keep a sharp eye open to avoid collisions. The lead aircraft were equipped with Gee and were expected to drop flares and incendiaries onto the target area. The following aircraft would bomb on the flares and fires rather than trying to find the target themselves.

Operation Millennium took place on the night of 26 May 1942, though Cologne was bombed instead of Hamburg due to last minute weather problems. Although the 1,047 bombers straggled somewhat, the aim was better than on previous raids and losses were lighter – at around 4%. On 1 June a thousand bomber force was sent to Essen, and to Bremen on 25 June. Thereafter no such heavy raids could be mounted. The effort had so disrupted normal bombing missions and training schedules that Bomber Command was staggering under the workload. Nevertheless, the merits of streaming, target marking and planned routes to and from targets had been proved. The days of the self-sufficient bomber finding its way to and from a target were over.

From this date to the end of the war, Bomber Command followed a fairly consistent daily routine. At 9 am Air Chief Marshal Harris and his senior officers left breakfast in the officers' mess at Bomber Command HQ at Walter's Ash in Buckinghamshire – where a fine bust of Harris still stands – and walked over the road to the Operations Room. There they were given a briefing on any operations flown the previous night. At around 10 am a meteorological officer gave a weather forecast for all of western Europe. Harris and his officers then compared this against the list of targets, taking into account the latest intelligence, aerial photographs and any special requests from the government, navy, army or others. By noon, Harris had decided which targets – if any – to attack that night as well as how many aircraft should be sent out from which Group. This information was then sent to the Group HQs, where detailed planning of routes, streaming and

The twin towers of Cologne Cathedral rise above the rubble of the city centre. The cathedral managed to survive the devastation of the thousand bomber raid almost unscathed, though the nave was to be damaged in later attacks on the city.

other details was carried out. By mid-afternoon the squadron commanders knew how many aircraft they had to send and the details of the mission. Crews were then chosen, and instructed to take their aircraft on short test flights. In early evening the crews were called for a final briefing. At dusk the bombers took off, forming up at a designated spot over England into their streams and heading for the enemy skies.

For the rest of the war there would be little change in the way Bomber

Command operated. The scale and ferocity of the raids would, however, increase out of all recognition.

One of the problems that was to worry aircrew for the rest of the war, due to the increased number of bombers, was the risk of collision. On dark, moonless nights it was almost impossible to spot another black painted aircraft showing no lights even at close range.

Another problem was being hit by bombs dropped by aircraft higher up, as was found by Sergeant James Williams when piloting his 35th raid on 2 July 1942 over Bremen. He had just let his bombs drop when the port wing of his Wellington was hit by a stick of incendiaries from another aircraft. Most bounced off after inflicting various dents and holes, but one bomb got caught in the air intake of the port engine. Seconds later it went off, setting fire to engine and wing alike. Williams

The wedding of Sergeant Francis Pickering of No 107 Squadron to Sissy Joan in May 1942. Five months later Pickering was shot down over Holland. (Massingham MHSSLRAFMM)

threw the aircraft around the sky in a desperate attempt to dislodge the bomb. Eventually the incendiary fell free, after which the engine fire was put out with the onboard extinguisher. The damaged bomber limped home to Marham without further incident.

Technical innovations continued to be installed throughout 1942. One of these was the Lorenz system by which an aircraft could be landed even in the worst weather conditions. Sadly it was not infallible, as Squadron Leader (later Wing Commander) Arthur Ashworth recalled:

'After an attack on Düsseldorf on the night of the 31st July we were returning at low level when we spotted a train and stopped it by spraying the engine liberally from both front and rear turrets. When we got back to base from this sortie there was fog on the ground and we were instructed to divert to the North, but, being confident of my ability to land using the 'Lorenz' system, I told ground control that I was coming in anyway and asked the navigator to switch to the relevant beam frequency.

Taken on 8th March 1942, this photograph shows the Boston Bombers of No 107 Squadron drawn up for a formal visit by civilian 'bigwigs' at Great Massingham.

Douglas DB-7 Boston

Type:	Medium bomber
Engines:	2 x 1600 hp
	Wright R-2600
	Double Cyclone
Wingspan:	61 ft 4 in
Length:	47 ft 6 in
Height:	17 ft 7 in
Weight:	Empty 15,051 lb
	Loaded 20,230 lb
Armament:	7 x 0.303 in machine guns in nose, ventral and dorsal positions
Bomb-load:	2,000 lb of bombs
Max speed:	338 mph
Ceiling:	27,600 ft
Range:	745 miles
Production:	7,385

The Douglas Boston was originally designed in 1939 to be a tactical strike aircraft for the French. The British took over the orders for the early aircraft, then demanded that the aircraft be redesigned to give it a longer range, which was needed to cross the North Sea. At first the RAF allocated its Bostons to the Free French crews who were familiar with it, but as the performance style of the aircraft became better known it was gradually adopted by British and Commonwealth squadrons in place of their Blenheims. The Boston was also produced in a nightfighter version, known as the Havoc.

'The system consists of a fixed narrow beam which, when the aircraft is correctly aligned, gives a continuous tone signal. Deviation from the beam to one side results in dots being heard, while dashes appear when off the beam on the other side. There are also the warning signals from an outer and an inner marker and, at the source of transmission, a cone of silence.

'I timed the beam, a procedure from which one could learn the direction from oneself of the transmitter, and then joined the beam. I was a bit nonplussed when I found that the beam I was flying did not appear to be

Lockheed PV-1/B-34 Ventura

Type:	Medium bomber
Engines:	2 x 1850 hp Pratt & Whitney R-2800 Double Wasp
Wingspan:	65 ft 6 in
Length:	51 ft 9 in
Height:	11 ft 11 in
Weight:	Empty 20,197 lb Loaded 31,077 lb
Armament:	4 x 0.5 in machine guns in nose and dorsal turret, plus 2 x 0.303 in machine guns in ventral position
Bomb-load:	3,000 lb of bombs
Max speed:	322 mph
Ceiling:	26,300 ft
Range:	1,660 miles
Production:	2,475

The Ventura was a bomber version of the tried and tested Lodestar transport aircraft which had been flying since 1938. It was ordered by the RAF in the summer of 1940 and deliveries began two years later. The Ventura proved vulnerable to German fighters when used on daylight raids and before long was largely handed over to Coastal Command for long distance patrol work. The majority of the Venturas served in the Pacific theatre against the Japanese where their long range and heavy bomb-load made them useful for attacking isolated islands.

aligned on the same compass heading as I had expected, but I put this down, wrongly, to a cross wind. Eventually, having checked the outer and inner markers and the cone of silence, I started my approach. We passed over the outer marker at the correct height and let down at the stipulated rate of descent to cross the inner marker. Shortly after this the flarepath lights should have appeared and, sure enough, a line of lights shone through the fog on our port side and I set the aircraft down. Immediately there were marked movements by the aircraft and she showed that she was unhappy

Focke Wulf Fw 190

Type:	Fighter
Engines:	1700 hp BMW801D
Wingspan:	34 ft 5 in
Length:	29 ft
Height:	13 ft
Weight:	Empty 6,393 lb
	Loaded 8,770 lb
Armament:	2 x 7.9 mm machine guns in nose plus 4 x 20 mm cannon in wings
Max speed:	382 mph
Ceiling:	35,000 ft
Range:	497 miles
Production:	20,051 of all models

When the Focke Wulf Fw 190 first appeared in combat over France in 1941 it came as a rude shock to the RAF, as it was so clearly superior to any other fighter in the world. It was not until the end of 1942 when the Spitfire X entered service that the Allies were able to match the superlative performance of this aircraft. So successful was the Fw190 that the Germans soon began producing a number of variants, including ground-attack, long-range escort and fighter bomber.

with the state of the surface on which she had been landed and there was a general indication of rough ground.

'I concluded that our airfield had been bombed and informed my crew to that effect. Because the navigator had selected the wrong frequency and I had been somewhat careless in my assumptions, we had landed off the runway of the newly finished airfield at Lakenheath, some miles from our base and the ground surrounding the runway had yet to be consolidated.

'Shortly after that, a sign appeared on the door of OC 'A' Flight. It read:
ASHWORTH & CO - AVIATORS
TRIPS TO 'HAPPY VALLEY' AT GOVERNMENT EXPENSE
Some low type subsequently inserted below this:
"Return Trip Not Guaranteed."'

Chapter 6

Regrouping to Attack

In **August 1942** there took place a reorganisation in Bomber Command which was to have a profound effect on the future of the war, though it did not seem like that at the time and certainly was only marginal to the fighting experiences of the men serving in Norfolk.

For some months it had been becoming increasingly clear to the higher command that only some crews could be relied upon to find targets consistently and bomb them accurately, even with the new navigational equipment entering service. As we have seen, it had therefore become usual to assign these crews to the task of flying slightly ahead of the main bomber stream on a raid. They would bomb the target with flares or incendiaries to mark it clearly for the following bomb-aimers. Air Chief Marshal Harris, as Commander-in-Chief of Bomber Command, left the choice of which crews from which squadrons should do the marking to his Group staff, or even to individual squadron commanders, on the grounds that they knew the crews and conditions over the targets best.

However, the staff at the Air Ministry disagreed. Group Captain Bufton, Director of Bomber Operations, was increasingly of the view that marking a target was such a specialised skill that it demanded a type of individual training that was not available to crews on bomber squadrons. He wanted to form a Target Marking Force of four squadrons which would be specially trained for this sole task.

Following the reorganisation of Bomber Command, specialist training units were established. The Oxford was used as a trainer to accustom pilots to how twin-engined aircraft behaved in flight.

The row between Harris and Bufton rumbled on for weeks. Finally Sir Charles Portal, Chief of the Air Staff, backed Bufton. The new force was, however, given the name suggested by Harris: The Pathfinders.

The Pathfinders were based at Wyton, outside Norfolk, but their work was to have a huge impact on the men from Norfolk bombing Germany. And the establishment of the force would pave the way for the later formation of the specialised No 100 Group, which would be based in the county.

Of rather more immediate effect in Norfolk was the arrival of a revolutionary new aircraft, the Mosquito. At first this aircraft was kept secret, but when it did become public knowledge a special documentary film was made about it for cinema release, so frantic was public interest. Made entirely of wood, the Mosquito was produced by the de Havilland company as a private venture after the government turned it down in 1938. But the first prototype flight in 1940 was so spectacular that the RAF ordered it in numbers. The wood chosen was balsa, a special very strong wood from South America which was incredibly light and so suitable for aircraft.

The new aircraft was given to No 105 Squadron and, after a few minor

Mosquitos of No 105 Squadron lined up at RAF Marham for a press visit. The 'Wooden Wonder', as the Mosquito came to be known, was a source of great fascination for the media.

Ground crew refuel a No 105 Squadron Mosquito. On some days a replacement crew would take up a Mosquito while its usual crew rested, allowing each aircraft to fly two missions to Germany within 24 hours.

raids, made a spectacular entrance to the war on 30 January 1943. Three Mosquitos led by Squadron Leader R.W. Reynolds set off on a flight to Berlin that took them mostly over the sea at very low level to avoid German radar. As they crossed the coast, the Mosquitos climbed rapidly to 25,000 feet to arrive over Berlin at exactly 11 am. At that moment Reichsmarschall Hermann Goering, head of the Luftwaffe, stood up to make a speech to a Nazi rally. The RAF Mosquitos scattered bombs around, which disrupted the meeting live on radio to great propaganda effect.

Rather less successful was an attack on Oslo on 25 September 1942. The raid was aimed at the Gestapo HQ for occupied Norway and timed to coincide with a rally by Norwegian Nazis. The Mosquitos evaded German defences, but had the misfortune to be spotted by a patrolling force of Focke Wulf Fw 190s. The Germans dived down and succeeded in shooting down a Mosquito just as the force was making its bombing run. The aim of the survivors was disrupted so that, although they dropped all their bombs within 100 yards of the Gestapo HQ, the rally was not actually hit.

This was also the time that the Wellington was finally being phased out of operational duties in Europe, though it continued to fly in other theatres of the war. At East Wretham No 115 Squadron was re-equipped with the superlative Lancaster, while other squadrons received Stirlings.

No 218 Squadron was one of those given Stirlings. Like other airmen, they found the Stirling a reliable and tough aircraft, but one that could not be coaxed above 17,000 feet with its bombs on board. Some crews turned a necessity into an advantage by choosing to return home at a low level in the hopes of avoiding the Luftwaffe nightfighters which tended to prowl at altitude to prey on the bomber streams. While coming back from a raid on Fallersleben on 13 December 1942, rear gunner Sergeant Gilbert Holland spotted no fewer than three railway trains parked in sidings. He called up the pilot and persuaded him to come around to attack, even though the Stirling

A flight of Stirlings of No 218 Squadron operating out of Marham early in 1942. At first hailed as a decisive new weapon, the Stirling would soon prove itself to be unable to fly at altitude.

Winston Churchill visits RAF East Wretham on 6 June 1941. To Churchill's left in a homberg hat is Clement Attlee, then Deputy Prime Minister and leader of the Labour Party. (Massingham MHSSLRAFMM)

had no bombs left on board. Instead, Holland and the other gunners raked the trains with machine gun fire from low level, causing one locomotive to explode and no doubt inflicting great damage on whatever cargo the trains were carrying.

All new aircraft are prone to teething troubles, but for the men who were putting their lives at risk such problems could be deadly. Men in combat are prey to superstition, and the crews of RAF Bomber Command were no exception. It soon began to be whispered around the bases of Bomber Command that a new species of fairies or goblins were at work, making perfectly good equipment suddenly go wrong for no apparent reason. They went by the name of gremlins and were widely blamed for all sorts of technical problems.

A typical gremlin incident affected a bomber sent out on 13 March 1943. Charles Dear explains:

'Half an hour out from base it was realised that no response was forthcoming from the mid upper gunner. I went back to investigate and found him unconscious in his turret. Of all places most difficult to evacuate a body it was the mid upper turret of a Lancaster. It is above head height with the gunner sitting on a swing seat which I had to prise from under his bottom and ease him down onto my shoulder. Alone in the dark and at 20,000 ft this was not easy and it took me 20 minutes and the use of three emergency oxygen bottles to achieve. During the process the gunner was sick over me which fortunately froze and gentle patting of my flying suit caused the vomit to cascade to the floor as crystals. Since we had already lost the use of our navigation set (Gee) and not knowing the cause of the gunner's sickness the captain decided to abandon the sortie. We therefore blew some holes in the sea and returned to base. It later transpired that the oxygen tube to the mid upper turret had become disconnected, not helpful for the gunner.'

Taken rather more seriously by the higher echelons of the RAF were the 'foo fighters'. These began to be seen in numbers as the bomber offensive increased in intensity. They took the form of small glowing balls of light, perhaps two feet or so across, that flew alongside the bombers as they droned through the air. At first it was thought that the strange lights were a German weapon, so air gunners fired at them whenever they appeared. However, the foo fighters did not explode or attack, so it was then supposed that they were a German surveillance device of some kind. This idea too was discounted when it was realised that formations that attracted foo fighters were no more likely to be attacked than those that did not. After the war it was discovered that the Germans were as mystified by the foo fighters as the British. Luftwaffe nightfighter pilots had seen and reported the odd lights flying alongside bombers, and presumed them to be some British device. The mystery has never been solved.

While some squadrons were gaining new aircraft, others kept on with their existing stock. The Ventura was, by this time, proving to be vulnerable so many crews practised low flying in the hope that this would protect them from Luftwaffe fighters. For one crew it was the training that proved fatal. On 10 December 1942 a No 21 Squadron Ventura suddenly had an engine explode over Methwold Hyde. Local resident Wes Wortley heard the bang and looked up to see the aircraft, a ball of flame, passing low overhead. It crashed a short distance away and Wortley ran to see if he could help.

There were no survivors. All Wortley found was a burning wreck and a mass of wreckage and debris. Among it was a photograph of a small girl. The photo had no writing on it and although he took it to the squadron,

The combined aircrew of No 107 Squadron, photographed at Great Massingham in the spring of 1942 as the squadron completed its transfer from Blenheims to Bostons. (Massingham MHSSLRAFMM)

nobody was able to identify the child nor to which of the dead crewmen it had belonged. He kept it for years, hoping to reunite it with its rightful owner. After Wortley's death the photo passed to his nephew, Chris Cock. If anyone can identify the photo, Chris can be contacted via the Feltwell Historical Society on www.feltwell.org.

More successful as a combat aircraft was the Boston, flown by No 107 Squadron out of Great Massingham. Among the more specific and less usual targets to be attacked was a ship bringing whale oil into Cherbourg in September. The RAF had been tipped off about the ship by the Resistance and No 107 was sent to attack. Pilot Officer Wallace Martin from Australia won a DFC for the cool way he dived on the target, sinking the ship with a well aimed bomb.

In December 1942 the first tests of a new navigational aid were held. Oboe was far more precise than was the earlier Gee, pinpointing an aircraft's

The battered photograph of a young girl found beside a crashed RAF aircraft in December 1942. The identity of the girl became an enduring enigma around RAF Feltwell that came to sum up the tragedy of war. (www.feltwell.org)

The four-man crew of Boston 'M-Mother' of No 107 Squadron, photographed beside their aircraft at Great Massingham, in early 1943. (Massingham MHSSLRAFMM)

position to just a few yards, although it was effective only at fairly limited range from Britain. Nevertheless it could be used by the Pathfinders to mark a large target even when dense cloud covered the entire area. The system worked by equipment in the aircraft receiving, then retransmitting, signals from bases in Britain. This allowed greater accuracy than the passive receivers of Gee. A signal from Britain kept the bomber flying on a set course and informed the bomb-aimer when he was directly over his target.

Meanwhile, the Germans had found a way to jam Gee so the search was on for a navigational aid for the mass of bombers. The answer came with H2S, said to be derived from the phrase 'Home Sweet Home' as it could lead a crew back to base. This was a small radar set mounted in the bomber and pointed downward. Working on the 10 cm wavelength, the radar could

A Boston of No 107 Squadron operating out of RAF Great Massingham. Fast and manoeuvrable, the Boston proved to be ideal for the low-level daylight attacks being carried out by No 2 Group at this time. (Massingham MHSSLRAFMM)

distinguish open water from land and countryside from built-up areas. It was good enough to give the navigator operating it a reasonably accurate view of what lay beneath any clouds and match it to his charts. As of January 1943, H2S was fitted to all new four-engine bombers, though older aircraft remained without it.

The spring of 1943 saw other changes. The previously rather haphazard system of tours of duty was now formalised. A first tour lasted 30 operational missions, after which the aircrew were rested for a minimum of six months

Nobby Clark and his crew from No 107 Squadron stand in front of their Douglas Boston parked on the grassy airfield of RAF Great Massingham in the summer of 1943. (Massingham MHSSLRAFMM)

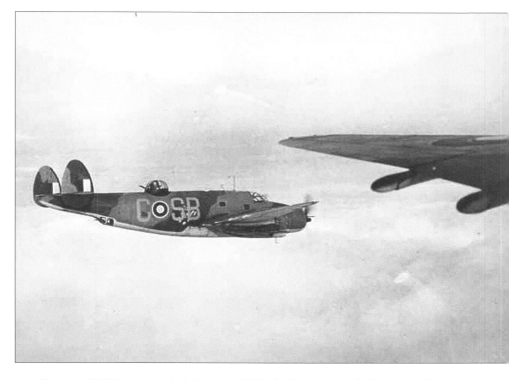

Ventura AE939 on a sortie in January 1943. It flew a total of 19 sorties with No 464 Squadron prior to a landing accident on 11 May, 1943. Like most other Venturas at this date it carries artwork underneath the aircraft code that was applied by the Disney artists at the factory in Burbank, California. Walt Disney himself encouraged his artists to do this in their off time as the factory was next door to his studios! (www.feltwell.org)

doing desk jobs or training others. A second tour of 20 missions was then expected, after which aircrew were no longer required to return to combat. The survival rate of a full two tours was around 40% at this time.

On 5 March, 'Bomber' Harris began the offensive that he had been planning all through the winter when bad weather had kept most of Bomber Command's squadrons on the ground. The Battle of the Ruhr was designed to crush that part of western Germany as an effective industrial area. Large-scale area bombing was intended to destroy factories, flatten homes and so severely disrupt the transport system that few materials could get in any

Wing Commander John Wooldridge, the commanding officer of No 105 Squadron for most of 1943, sits perched on the canopy of his Mosquito. Wooldridge left the RAF after the war to carve out a new career as a scriptwriter of drama on radio and then the newfangled television.

In April 1943 the station commander of RAF Marham, Group Captain Wallace Kyle, explains a point to aircrew of No 105 Squadron. Kyle rose to the rank of Air Chief Marshal after the war.

more than finished weapons could get out. The battle would last until July, by which time Harris accepted that German defences had been strengthened to such an extent that any damage inflicted was no longer worth the loss.

One man who survived the Battle of the Ruhr was Sergeant Leonard Bird, an air gunner with No 218 Squadron who had a remarkable career. He was a regular RAF man from before the war who had spent some months fighting in North Africa using the Wellesley bomber, considered obsolete for European flying but good enough when facing the Italians in what is now Ethiopia, but was then Abyssinia. In February 1941, after several successful sorties, Bird's aircraft was shot down in flames. He managed to bale out but was taken prisoner.

In April 1941 the Italians in Abyssinia surrendered and Sergeant Bird returned to his squadron, No 47. In June 1942 he moved to No 218 Squadron in England and on only his second sortie shot down a German nightfighter over Bremen. Two months later his aircraft accidentally caught fire just 15 minutes after take-off. Again he baled out as flames engulfed his guns but this time he landed in England and next day was back with

A Ventura being bombed-up at RAF Feltwell. Note the empty bomb trolley in the left foreground and the woman driver of the tractor that has been pulling the bombs. (www.feltwell.org)

No 218. No wonder his CO recommended him for the DFM, stating, 'He has shown exceptional keenness and this, coupled with his wide experience of operations, has been a splendid example to the younger gunners in the squadron.' Sergeant Bird got his medal in April, on completing his 60th combat flight.

In May an observer of No 115 Squadron on his 23rd operation, Sergeant Jack Cope, was shot down over Nuremburg. He managed to bale out of the stricken Lancaster bomber, landing in a field. He was unable to find his colleagues, so he set off alone trying to get as far as possible from the crashed aircraft before dawn in the hope of evading capture by the Germans. One month later, Cope presented himself to a rather surprised sentry at the gate giving access from Spain to Gibraltar. He never revealed exactly how he had managed to get across Europe so as to protect those who had helped him from German reprisals.

Throughout the Battle of the Ruhr, the RAF continued to attack other targets. One raid went disastrously wrong, but ended with the awarding of a Victoria Cross to its leader, Squadron Leader Leonard Trent of No 487 Squadron.

A crew of No 107 Squadron prepare their Boston for combat in May 1943. Pilot J.P. Crump is perched on the wing; Gunner Sergeant Verrier sits at his guns while Wireless Operator Dotteridge stands on the ground.

On 3 May Squadron Leader Trent was briefed at Methwold to take twelve Venturas from No 487 Squadron to attack the power station at Amsterdam. The power station was crucial to war industries in the area, and it was also hoped that its destruction would be a major morale boost to the Dutch workers, who were then undertaking a series of strikes aimed at causing trouble for the German occupiers. Because the defences were expected to be fairly heavy, Trent decided to fly low all the way with his aircraft arranged in two formations of six aircraft each. He was also given two squadrons of Spitfires to act as close support.

The Venturas left Methwold at around 4.30 pm with Squadron Leader Trent in the lead aircraft along with Flight Lieutenant V. Phillips as navigator, Flying Officer Roy Thomas as wireless operator and Sergeant W. Trenery as gunner. Almost at once the Ventura 'Q' with Sergeant Barker at the controls had part of its canopy blown off and was forced to return to Methwold. Meanwhile, the Spitfires appeared and closed up at low level while the bombers roared over the coast towards Amsterdam.

Unknown to the British, the German Governor of the Netherlands was on an official visit to Haarlem. In case news of this had leaked out, the Luftwaffe had put up a protective formation of 70 Messerschmitt Bf 109s and Focke Wulf Fw 190s. Trent's route was to take him just five miles from Haarlem.

Unaware of the danger, Squadron Leader Trent crossed the Dutch coast and began to climb to the bombing height of 12,000 feet. The Luftwaffe spotted the formation at the same moment and, assuming it was heading for Haarlem, sent their fighters to intercept. The Focke Wulfs pounced first, but were attacked by the Spitfires so effectively that none got through to the Venturas. The slower Messerschmitts arrived next, and finding the Spitfires busily engaged headed straight for the bombers.

Almost at once the aircraft 'C' Charlie was hit. The pilot, Flight Lieutenant A. Duffill, turned for home with both engines on fire and his gunner wounded. Simultaneously two other Venturas went down, then a few minutes later three more. Squadron Leader Trent led his formation in evasive manoeuvres, then returned to his course towards Amsterdam. The Germans, momentarily shaken off, attacked again and shot down two more Venturas. Trent's aircraft evened the score slightly by downing a Bf 109. That left just Trent and two others boring in towards the power station.

Flak opened up, forcing one of the remaining three Venturas to pull out of the attack with a burning engine. The two aircraft dropped their bombs

Glen Stewart of No 107 Squadron takes up his position as air gunner in his Boston aircraft. The exposed position and twin guns of the dorsal gunner position on the Boston was considered old-fashioned by this date, but the speed and handling of the bomber made up for the lack of firepower. (Massingham MHSSLRAFMM)

accurately, but the second Ventura was shot to pieces at almost the same instant that a flak shell exploded inside the fuselage of Squadron Leader Trent's aircraft. All the controls instantly went dead, so Trent ordered his crew to bale out. As he struggled to keep the stricken aircraft level so that his crew could get out, it was hit again. The explosion threw Trent out of the cockpit. As he fell to earth he saw the shattered fragments of his bomber diving to destruction. He opened his parachute, and was captured within minutes of landing in a ploughed field just outside Amsterdam.

Back at Methwold, the squadron nervously awaited news. Sergeant Barker's aircraft had returned damaged some time earlier, and the Spitfire leader had radioed back that the formation was under heavy attack. The last the Spitfires had seen was the Ventura formation heading on to Amsterdam while they fought off the Focke Wulfs. Flight Lieutenant Duffell limped home in 'C' Charlie some time later, reporting the Messerschmitt attack and loss of two Venturas. Since then there had been no news. It was not until many hours later that the men and women waiting so anxiously at Methwold had to accept that no other Venturas were coming home that day.

Two weeks later King George VI and Queen Elizabeth, later the Queen Mother, insisted on breaking their schedule when nearby to visit Methwold to meet all surviving aircrew of No 487 squadron, and to speak to the ground crew and other station staff.

Flight Lieutenant Duffill was presented with a DFC for the action, and his navigator, Frederick Starkie, was also awarded the DFC. Alan Turnbull, the wounded gunner in Duffill's aircraft, was presented with a DFM by the King. As soon as the Bf 109s attacked, Turnbull had left his position as wireless operator to occupy the astrodome and act as fight controller, spotting the approaching enemy aircraft and directing the gunner's aim. After the damaged aircraft left formation, Turnbull moved to the ventral gun position to operate the two guns there. He kept firing until a hail of cannon shells knocked out both guns and badly injured his legs. Undeterred by the pain, Turnbull proceeded to put out the fire that had been started before passing out.

Meanwhile the upper gunner, Sergeant Lawrence Neill, had also been injured by the cannon fire. He gave Turnbull first aid before returning to his guns to shoot down a Luftwaffe fighter and drive off the rest – thus probably saving the lives of himself and his comrades. Like Turnbull, Sergeant Neill was awarded a DFM.

Squadron Leader Trent spent the rest of the war as a prisoner in Germany.

On the release of himself and the other 17 survivors of the raid he was awarded the Victoria Cross. Trent remained in the RAF after the war, retiring in 1965 to return to his home in New Zealand. Although RAF Methwold has long since been demolished, much of the site is now covered by housing and light industrial units, and one of the residential roads is named Trent VC Close.

In June No 98 Squadron took off from Foulsham to bomb Capriquet aerodrome near Caen in France. These raids into France, like those into other occupied countries, were always difficult. The Germans often had their most valuable targets in or near French towns, and the British government was always keen to avoid causing the deaths of French civilians. As a result such raids were usually carried out in daylight and at low level in an attempt to get as great a degree of accuracy as possible.

Sergeant Glendinning Colkett was bomb-aimer in one of the aircraft and, like his fellows, had been briefed repeatedly about the need to avoid civilian casualties. As the aircraft came in to attack, a flak shell exploded just below the aircraft, sending a red hot shard of metal up through the floor of the bomber and into Colkett's leg. Despite this, he calmly kept his eye glued to the bombsights and dropped his bombs accurately. It was not until they were over the Channel and on the way home, free from enemy defences, that Colkett bothered his pilot with the news that he was injured. With some understatement his squadron commander wrote, 'he has set a fine example to other bomb aimers'.

Quite different problems were encountered by those squadrons sent to attack distant targets. Among these was No 105 Squadron, flying its Mosquitos out of Marham. On 27 May 1943 six Mosquitos were sent to attack targets at Jena, in eastern Germany. As usual, the bombers flew out at low level over the North Sea, then struck inland, tearing across the landscape at high speed and near the ground.

As the formation approached Jena the weather deteriorated sharply – forecasting the weather far to the east was a perennial problem for the RAF. Mist and low cloud reduced visibility to just 800 yards, which was not much in an aircraft that could cover that distance in under 17 seconds. Light flak had begun to come up when suddenly balloons were seen, their deadly cables running up from the ground ready to slice the wing off any aircraft that struck them. The aircraft climbed rapidly to evade the danger and at once the target was lost in the murk below. One man, Sergeant Leslie Hogan, thought he knew where the target was. Rather than turn for the

de Havilland Mosquito

Type:	Light bomber
Engines:	2 x 1480 hp Rolls-Royce Merlin 21
Wingspan:	54 ft 2 in
Length:	40 ft 11 in
Height:	15 ft 3 in
Weight:	Empty 14,900 lb
	Loaded 22,380 lb
Armament:	none
Bomb-load:	2,000 lb of bombs
Max speed:	415 mph
Ceiling:	36,000 ft
Range:	1,795 miles
Production:	1,159 (out of 6,535 Mosquitos of all variants)

The Mosquito would later be produced in fighter, fighter-bomber and photo-reconnaissance versions, but its first role was as a bomber. What made the Mosquito unique was that it relied on its high speed and fantastic handling, rather than on guns, to escape defences. It ended the war with the lowest loss rate of any bomber by a wide margin. It was first delivered to the RAF in autumn 1941, but did not enter operations until May 1942 due to delays and difficulties in training bomber crews how to use it to the best of its abilities. The 'wooden wonder', as it was known, remained in production until 1950.

long journey home having achieved nothing, the men of No 105 dived back into the mist and cloud following the calmly reassuring directions of Hogan. Miraculously the target was exactly where he said it was. Bombs gone, the Mosquitos tore off for home.

A 105 Squadron Mosquito flies past RAF Marham at low level. The ability of the Mosquito to fly long distances at low level made it a superlative weapon, but demanded intense concentration from the crew.

Avro Lancaster

Type:	Heavy bomber
Engines:	Model B1 4 x 1280 hp
	Rolls-Royce Merlin Mk20
	Model B2 4 x 1675 hp
	Bristol Hercules VI
Wingspan:	102 ft
Length:	68 ft 10 in
Height:	20 ft 4 in
Weight:	Empty 41,000 lb
	Loaded 68,000 lb
Armament:	8 x 0.303 in machine guns, 2 in nose turret,
	2 in dorsal turret, 4 in tail turret
Bomb-load:	14,000 lb
Max speed:	287 mph
Ceiling:	24,500 ft
Range:	2,678 miles
Production:	7,377

The Lancaster was the most successful British bomber of the Second World War. It was developed by Avro from the earlier Manchester, the two engines of which proved to be seriously underpowered. The addition of two extra engines meant the aircraft required longer wings, but otherwise it remained effectively the same. The first prototype flew on 9 January 1941 and production began that October. The first aircraft was delivered to an operational squadron in March 1942, but engine shortages meant it was many months before the machine was available in large numbers. As well as the standard B1 and B2 models, the Lancaster was produced in a variety of special configurations, most notably the 23 aircraft built with larger bomb bays and no dorsal turret to undertake the Dambuster Raid. After the war, large numbers of Lancasters were converted to Lincoln passenger aircraft or Lancastrian cargo carriers and sold off to a variety of airlines in many different countries. Today only one Lancaster remains in flying condition, and is with the RAF Battle of Britain Flight, but a number of others are able to taxi and several are on static display in museums.

Chapter 7

The Gomorrah Raid

According to the Book of Genesis, the people of the city of Gomorrah, and its neighbour Sodom, committed an abomination in the eyes of the Lord due to their wickedness. 'Then the Lord rained upon Sodom and Gomorrah brimstone and fire out of Heaven and He overthrew those cities. ... And Abraham looked toward Sodom and Gomorrah, and toward all the land of the plain, and beheld and lo, the smoke of the country went up as the smoke of a furnace.'

Air Chief Marshal Sir Arthur Harris, Commander-in-Chief of Bomber Command, knew his Bible. So when he chose the name 'Operation Gomorrah' for his next major assault on Germany, it boded badly for the target that he chose: Hamburg.

Hamburg was the second largest city in Germany after Berlin and the most important industrial area outside the Ruhr. The city had already been attacked over 90 times by Bomber Command, but with only indifferent results. Now Harris decided to put all the lessons learned so far, plus the new aircraft and technology, to good effect. He intended to launch a series of major raids by massed formations of heavy bombers to overwhelm the defences and flatten large areas of the city.

The first raid took place on 24 July 1943 when 790 aircraft were concentrated in a stream that took just 50 minutes to pass over the city. This was the first time that a new weapon was used: Window. Window consisted of thousands of strips of aluminium foil dropped by aircraft sent out ahead of and on the flanks of the bomber stream. As the foil fell to earth it jammed German radar, making it impossible for the air controllers to guide Luftwaffe nightfighters to the bombers. Losses among the bombers were light at just 1.5%. The raid caused much damage to the docks and city centre.

It was on this raid that Sergeant John Parkinson of No 218 Squadron got the fright of his life. He was flight engineer on his Lancaster, code letter J, when a 30 lb incendiary bomb crashed through the roof, having been dropped by another bomber higher up in the stream. Parkinson scooped up the bomb and threw it out of the aircraft, which then continued on its mission without further incident.

For the next two nights Hamburg was subjected to nuisance raids by Mosquitos of No 139 Squadron operating from Marham. Then, on 27 July the main bomber force returned. This time the weaker Stirlings carried incendiaries to allow them to gain height and keep up with the faster Lancasters. Hamburg had been basking in a long spell of dry weather and the bombing of the previous raid had smashed buildings, scattering rafters and floorboards across the dry city. Hamburg was a tinderbox. The raid was the spark.

The fires began in the damaged blocks of flats and apartments in the eastern part of the city centre. As the flames took hold, the hot air began to rise, sucking in fresh cool air from the surrounding area. This oxygen-rich wind fanned the flames at gale force. A fire-storm was created in which temperatures rose to such an extent that anything that could burn did. A large area of the city was utterly destroyed and, although the death toll was never clearly known, as many as 40,000 people may have been killed. Around 800,000 were made homeless and refugees streamed out of the city.

The next night No 139 Squadron returned, followed 24 hours later by the main force again. This time the outer suburbs were hit and, although no firestorm was created, there was widespread destruction of housing. On 2 August another raid inflicted more damage.

The scale of damage was unprecedented. About two thirds of the city buildings had been destroyed, along with half the factories and almost all the port facilities. Albert Speer, Hitler's Minister of Armaments, visited the city. For the first time he began to believe that Germany could lose the war and estimated that if the RAF hit six more cities in like fashion, Germany would be unable to produce the weapons needed by its armed forces.

In the event, Bomber Command was never again able to repeat the awesome destruction visited on Hamburg. The circumstances that gave rise to the firestorm were unique to Hamburg that week, and German defences were soon improved markedly. In particular the Luftwaffe introduced what they called 'wild sow' nightfighters. These highly trained fighters followed the main bomber stream to its target, then used the light of exploding bombs and fires on the ground to locate and attack individual aircraft. Operating independently of ground-based radar, the wild sows were immune to Window. Bomber Command losses began to rise again.

One bomber to survive not just one, but two, wild sow attacks was a

The RAF cemetery at Feltwell occupies the northwest corner of the graveyard around the old, redundant church in the village. The graves cluster around a large monument dedicated to the memory of the men who flew from Feltwell and have no known grave.

Incendiary bombs being loaded into a Ventura of No 464 Squadron. By the date of the Gomorrah attacks the RAF had abandoned its crude pre-war incendiaries that consisted of little more than a five gallon drum of petrol with a small explosive charged strapped to the side. Instead the new phosphorous-benzol weapon, available in 4 lb and 30 lb sizes, was being used, based on a German bomb used on Coventry in 1940 that had failed to explode and been defused by the heroic men of the Bomb Disposal Squad. (www.feltwell.org)

Lancaster of No 115 Squadron attacking Mulheim as part of a stream of bombers. It was Sergeant Mason, the rear gunner, who saw the Messerschmitt Bf 110 first, alerting the pilot, Flying Officer Andrews, to the danger. The bomber was approaching the target and was silhouetted against the distant glow of searchlights and fires. The Messerschmitt shadowed the Lancaster for a few seconds, then dived to attack. Mason opened fire, causing the German to veer off after firing only a short, ineffective burst.

Seconds after the bombs were dropped, the upper gunner spotted a second wild sow, this time a Junkers Ju 88 high overhead. Again, the Lancaster was silhouetted against the glow of the target while the attacker was in the relative safety of darkness. The Junkers came down to the attack, pouring accurate fire at the bomber. Sergeant Mason and the upper gunner returned fire and had the satisfaction of seeing one of the German's engines burst into flames that grew to engulf the entire wing.

The Lancaster was itself badly hit. The port inner engine was on fire, and flames spread rapidly to the fuselage. Sergeant Mason abandoned his turret to help put out the fire in the fuselage, while Flying Officer Andrews put the Lancaster into a steep dive. The rush of air put out the engine fire, though the engine itself was now useless. Limping along on three engines at low level, the bomber got back to base long after the others from the squadron.

Cologne was another city to be hit repeatedly in an effort to reduce industrial output and render it useless as a transport link. A No 115 Squadron Lancaster was returning from a raid on Cologne when a pair of Focke Wulf Fw 190 fighters were sighted shadowing it from above and behind. The tail gunner calmly gave pilot Sergeant William Jolly instructions for evasive moves while he and the upper gunner, Sergeant Hall, repeatedly drove off attacks. After some 20 minutes of combat, one of the Fw 190s launched a swooping attack from behind and below that sliced the rear end off the Lancaster, hurling the unfortunate tail gunner to his death and setting the fuselage ablaze. The two Germans continued to attack, forcing Jolly to throw his battered aircraft into corkscrew turns while the hapless wireless operator, Sergeant Ray Crowther, was pitched around the burning fuselage trying to extinguish the fire. At one point, Crowther almost passed out when thrown against the hull. Sergeant Hall finally managed to hit one Fw 190, causing it to burst into flames, at which point the second German broke off. Although the aircraft was flying nose down due to the loss of weight at the rear and the tail controls were effectively useless, Sergeant Jolly got the battered aircraft back to England.

Meanwhile the twin-engine bombers continued their low level, daylight raids into occupied Europe. The Australian No 464 Squadron was still flying Venturas when it was ordered to undertake one of the notoriously dangerous 'ramrod' missions. The designation 'ramrod' meant that the need to hit the target was so urgent that at least one aircraft had to get through no matter how strong or effective the defences. This raid was on the rail viaduct at St Brieuc, a key transport link for the German forces manning the coastal defences of France. The formation was flying across the sea at low level under 5/10 cloud cover when a Focke Wulf Fw 190 dived down out of a cloud, having presumably been stalking the bombers for some time. Its target was the Ventura piloted by Flying Officer Wilbur Parsons.

The German opened fire immediately, raking the port wing to such effect that all controls were rendered useless. The gunner, Sergeant Brian McConnell, returned fire, but a hail of cannon shots ripped the canopy off, jammed the guns and literally blew him backwards to land heavily on the floor of the Ventura. Undeterred, McConnell scrambled back to his seat to watch the German's movements and give Flying Officer Parsons clear instructions on evasive manoeuvres. Although wounded in both hands, McConnell stayed in position until the Fw 190 gave up and left. Only then did he seek first aid, while Parsons piloted the crippled bomber back to England.

In August, Harris was ordered to pull his main force out of sorties over Germany in favour of attacks on Italian cities. Allied armies had invaded

Wing Commander Robert Young, the first commanding officer of No 464 Squadron, photographed at Feltwell in 1942. His Australian aircrews nicknamed him 'the Greek God' because of his supposed resemblance to a statue seen by some of them in a museum. (www.feltwell.org)

The Mosquitos of No 105 Squadron prepare to leave RAF Marham in July 1943. The squadron moved to Bourn, where it spent the remainder of the war.

Sicily and were poised to land in Italy itself. It was believed that a few heavy raids would induce Italy to surrender.

One such raid was undertaken on 12 August when the Stirlings of No 218 Squadron flew from Downham Market to bomb Turin, while a force of Halifaxes headed for Milan. The Stirling codemarked 'O' was piloted by Sergeant Arthur Aaron, who had already won a DFM for bringing his badly damaged bomber back from a raid on Germany. Sergeant Thomas Guy was wireless operator and Sergeant Allan Larden was bomb-aimer and second pilot, while Sergeant Malcolm Mitchem was flight engineer.

The long flight across France was uneventful and at just past 1 am, Sergeant Aaron manoeuvred over the Alps to take up his allotted position in the forming bomber stream. As he did so, the voice of upper gunner Sergeant J. Richmond came over the intercom. 'Watch that bloke up front, Art.' Another Stirling was visible to starboard, drifting slowly towards them. Aaron shifted the controls to avoid a collision. Then all hell broke loose.

The rear gunner on the other Stirling opened fire, raking Sergeant Aaron's aircraft from side to side along its wings. The navigator, Sergeant Bill Brennan, was killed instantly while Sergeant Larden received a bullet through his buttocks and Sergeant Mitchem's right boot was shot through three times without his foot being hit. Aaron was badly hit. One bullet shattered his jaw while two more had torn through his right arm and lodged in his chest. He collapsed forward over the control column, which sent the bomber hurtling down in a steep dive.

Sergeant Larden leapt into the second pilot's seat to grab the controls while Mitchem and Guy dragged Sergeant Aaron back into the fuselage. There the badly wounded pilot wrote a message instructing Larden to head for England, before he was given morphine and slipped into unconsciousness. With the hydraulic system destroyed and several control cables severed, it was all Larden could do to get the stricken bomber under control. By the time the Stirling was flying level, it was down to 4,000 feet and quite unable to recross the Alps. Larden headed south.

The men held a hurried conference about what to do. Baling out was ruled out as it would mean leaving Sergeant Aaron to die. It was decided to head for Sicily, and hope to find a place to land. Sergeant Guy began trying to raise a British air base in Sicily to ask permission to land while Sergeant Larden dumped the bombs on the naval base of La Spezia that fortuitously came into sight. Guy then managed to make contact with Bone in North Africa. He was ordered to navigate the bomber to Bone where emergency aid could be better given than on Sicily.

Four hours later the bomber crossed the African coast and Sergeant Larden was deeply relieved to see Bone come into view. Unfortunately Sergeant Guy then received a message that the runway was blocked by another aircraft that had crash-landed. The Stirling would have to put down on the rough ground alongside the runway. Not only was the land uneven, but it was very short, ending in a steep hill. As a second pilot, Larden was not really trained for this kind of difficult work. Doing his best, he manoeuvred round to line up. He was more than startled when the ghostly white face of Sergeant Aaron came into view as the wounded pilot resumed his seat.

Despite his appalling injuries, Aaron had decided to retake control of the aircraft. He had come out of his morphine-induced sleep to overhear the recent cockpit discussions and to feel the wallowing of the aircraft as Larden struggled.

Taking his seat, Sergeant Aaron had only one arm working and relied

Unidentified aircrew of No 105 Squadron pose in front of one of the squadron's Mosquitos at RAF Marham.

Bombs are loaded onto a No 105 Squadron Mosquito. The bomber version of the aircraft could carry 1,000 lbs of bombs in the bomb bay and, on shorter missions, an additional 500 lb bomb under each wing.

on Sergeant Larden to work the throttles. The first approach had to be abandoned due to the blocked runway. The second was abandoned when Aaron for some reason pulled up at the last minute. The third approach was made on virtually empty tanks. There would not be enough fuel for a fourth attempt. The bomber crashed heavily into the desert sand, skidding sideways until it came to a halt.

Emergency crews at once swarmed over the aircraft, spraying foam to douse any fires that might break out and dragging the crew off to hospital. It was only on leaving the Stirling that Sergeant Larden found that a bullet had hit his parachute harness. This had saved his life, but had rendered the parachute inoperable. If he had baled out he would have died. It was with great sadness that the crew heard that Sergeant Aaron died early that evening.

When writing to Sergeant Aaron's parents to tell them that their son had been awarded a posthumous Victoria Cross, Air Chief Marshal Harris wrote: 'In my opinion, never even in the annals of the RAF has the VC been awarded for skill, determination and courage in the face of the enemy of a higher order than that displayed by your son on his last flight.'

After the surrender of Italy, Harris put Bomber Command back to the task of attacking Germany by night with heavy bombers and nearer targets by day with lighter aircraft. Kassel was hit by a particularly heavy raid in October, but other cities continued to be attacked with smaller numbers of bombers.

Mannheim was raided in September by a relatively light force, among which was a Lancaster of No 115 Squadron from East Wretham piloted by Squadron Leader James Starky. As Mannheim came into view, the bomber was attacked by a Luftwaffe nightfighter which sprayed the aircraft with cannon shells and bullets. Instantly the great aircraft filled with smoke and pitched forward into a near vertical dive. After some tense seconds, Starky managed to drag the aircraft back to level flight, while an open window blew smoke out of the cockpit.

The surprisingly calm voice of Sergeant Willis, tail gunner, then came over the intercom to report that the German had followed them down and was now closing in for the kill. Sergeant Tugwell, the upper gunner, suggested that they pretend to be dead and wait until the enemy got closer. The German was misled by the stationary turrets and came in very close to the bomber. Then, to a shouted command, the two turrets sprang to life and poured a deadly hail of shot into the enemy fighter, which burst into flames and fell apart.

Meanwhile Squadron Leader Starky had realised that both the flight engineer and second pilot had been badly wounded. The bomb-aimer, Flying Officer Bernard Beer, dressed their wounds then volunteered to take over as flight engineer as well as doing his own duties as navigator. The bomber was now flying low and unable to regain height. A light flak battery opened up, but was silenced by a burst of fire from Sergeant Willis. Starky managed to nurse the aircraft back to England, crash-landing soon after crossing the coast.

As October 1943 came to a close, Bomber Command was in good shape. New tactics and new equipment were ensuring that raids were increasingly effective at hitting German war industries. The force was more powerful than it had ever been and its crews were becoming much more skilled in their tasks. Only the growing strength of the enemy's night defences continued to cause problems. Those problems were, however, great enough to prompt 'Bomber' Harris into making one of the few major changes to Bomber Command that enjoyed his full support. At the same time, the planning for an invasion of France the following year – D-Day – necessitated another change. Both reorganisations would have a profound impact on Bomber Command in Norfolk and the men who served there.

Short Stirling

Type:	Heavy bomber
Engines:	4 x 1650 hp Bristol Hercules XVI
Wingspan:	99 ft 1 in
Length:	87 ft 3 in
Height:	22 ft 9 in
Weight:	Empty 46,900 lb Loaded 70,000 lb
Armament:	8 x 0.303 in machine guns in nose, dorsal and tail turrets
Bomb-load:	14,000 lb of bombs
Max speed:	270 mph
Ceiling:	17,000 ft
Range:	2,010 miles
Production:	2,371 (Mks I, III, IV and V)

The Stirling got off to a bad start in May 1939 when the first prototype crashed on its maiden flight. Redesign followed, producing the final shape of this, the first four-engine bomber to enter service with the RAF. It started amid high hopes that it would prove to be a decisive aircraft for Bomber Command. It could carry a heavier bomb-load than any other aircraft in service and had a useful range, enabling it to reach many targets. Later in the war the low ceiling began to cause problems, as did the layout of the bomb bay which meant the Stirling could carry only smaller bombs. In 1943 the aircraft began to be replaced as a bomber. The existing Stirlings were converted to be glider tugs or long-distance transport aircraft.

Chapter 8

Foreign Heroes

Not all the men who fought in Bomber Command from Norfolk were British. A great many came from Empire and Commonwealth countries. Most of these men were at first integrated into the RAF, but later they formed their own squadrons. No 75 Squadron was composed chiefly of New Zealanders, as was No 487, while No 464 Squadron was recruited in Australia. Of course, these various servicemen were not really considered foreigners in 1939 – the Canadians, especially, were seen as part of the larger British family.

But there were some real foreigners flying in the RAF. In Norfolk there were two squadrons in particular composed of men who had no ties to Britain, but whose heroic help was much appreciated. The first was No 311 Squadron, which was formed on 29 July 1940, moving to East Wretham in September. This squadron was composed exclusively of Czech airmen who had managed to flee that unfortunate country after the German invasion of 1939.

At first these men had been based in France, officially fighting in the armed forces of the Czechoslovak government-in-exile of President Eduard Benes. When France fell to the Germans, the Czechs hastened to get to Britain. Those with aircraft flew out, taking as many of their ground crew as they could. Those on foot hijacked trucks and cars to get to western ports where the Royal Navy risked Luftwaffe bombers to take them off, along with isolated British units and other refugees.

When No 311 Squadron was formed, it was given new Wellington bombers to replace the Bloch 174 and Loiré 451 aircraft in which the Czechs had arrived in June 1940. The squadron continued to operate on Wellingtons out of East Wretham until April 1942 when it was transferred to Coastal Command and given the task of patrolling the North Sea to search for German ships and U-boats. In its time with Bomber Command, No 311 flew over a thousand operational sorties in 150 missions, dropping 1,300 tons of bombs on the enemy. The squadron's airmen were awarded no fewer than 18 DFCs, which was an impressive total given the number of men serving with the unit.

The outstanding figure of No 311 Squadron was Squadron Leader Josef Ocelka. As the squadron prepared to transfer to Coastal Command, the station commander was moved to write of him: 'He has always displayed conspicuous determination and devotion to duty and the recent successes of the squadron are in no small measure due to the high example he has set.'

A typical example of his dedication came on 28 March 1941 when he took off to attack Cologne. Soon after take-off the wireless died. When the wireless operator traced the fault he found that the entire electrical system of the bomber was in danger of failing. This was grounds for abandoning the mission, but Squadron Leader Ocelka refused to be put off. He flew on to reach and bomb Cologne. On the return trip, however, the navigator was unable to keep track of where the aircraft was. After crossing a stretch of open sea that Ocelka hoped was the English Channel, he spotted an airfield. He warily landed on the runway, but kept his engines running while he sent a crew member to find out where they were. Fortunately they were in England.

Like the Poles, the Czechs gained a well earned reputation for dashing bravery in action. Sadly, many of the men of No 311 Squadron did not live to return home, being killed in action. Several are buried in the churchyard of East Wretham, in a small corner reserved especially for them. Each year on Remembrance Sunday, the Czech government sends a representative to the village to lay a wreath by their graves.

Another foreign squadron within the RAF to operate out of Norfolk was No 342 (Lorraine) Squadron, composed of Free French fighters. Many thousands of French servicemen were in Britain when France surrendered to Germany in 1940. A part of the peace deal agreed between France and Germany was that all Frenchmen in Britain or the British Empire had to

The small group of Czech graves at East Wretham mark the presence in the village of No 311 Squadron, the only unit in Bomber Command to be composed almost exclusively of Czechs.

return home immediately, and those in the services would have to surrender to the Germans. However, one French officer in Britain – a tank commander by the name of General Charles de Gaulle – declared that as a former minister in the French government he was refusing to accept the surrender. Instead, de Gaulle declared, he was establishing an alternative Free French Government to continue the war and called upon all Frenchmen who were able to do so to join his new armed forces. The government in France responded by denouncing de Gaulle as a traitor and sentenced him to death. They made it clear that anyone who joined de Gaulle would also be regarded as a traitor.

The Frenchmen in Britain were, therefore, faced with a stark choice. They could go home to face life under German occupation, or stay in Britain and risk being treated as traitors if Germany won the war. To make things

Jacques Duchossy of No 342 (Lorraine) Squadron photographed (left) when serving in the French Air Force in 1939 and (right) when attending a reunion at Massingham in 2005. (Massingham MHSSLRAFMM)

worse, they were given only a few minutes to make up their minds. Perhaps understandably, most opted to go home and hope for peace. Only a minority chose to stay in Britain and fight on as part of the Free French forces. Of these, the airmen were mostly sent to the Middle East where they were able to operate from bases in former French colonies taken over by the British.

In 1943, as an Allied invasion of France became more of a possibility, the Free French were largely brought back to Britain. It was thought that they could be used to ease the path of the British and Americans as they entered France. In the meantime there was some serious fighting to do. Two Free French squadrons – Metz and Nancy – were merged to become No 342 Squadron RAF Bomber Command at Great Massingham. The new squadron was moved to West Raynham on 7 April 1943. By this date several French colonies had abandoned their allegiance to the regime in France and had recognised de Gaulle's Free French as the true government. Increasing numbers of Frenchmen were joining the Free French, swelling the numbers serving in units such as No 342 Squadron.

Among them was Pierre Mendes-France, who had served as a radical left-wing MP in France before the war. When his country surrendered, he was thrown into prison on the orders of the Germans. In 1941 he broke out of prison and fled over the Pyrenees to reach Gibraltar. He was then flown to Britain where he turned down the chance of serving in the Free French government in favour of joining a fighting force. Mendes-France survived the war to re-enter the French parliament as a radical left-winger. In June 1954 he became Prime Minister of France, but was ousted a year later and retired to the back benches. He remained in the French parliament until 1973, and died in 1982.

Among the lesser celebrities to serve with No 342 were Henri de Rancourt, then an unknown young officer but later the Chief of the French Air Force, and Generaux Gori, who rose to the rank of Chief Air Marshal in the 1960s.

The crew of a No 342 Squadron Boston pose beside their bomber. Like all Free French aircraft, ships and vehicles, this bomber is decorated with the Cross of Lorraine.

The officers of No 342 (Lorraine) Squadron photographed at Massingham in 1943.
(Massingham MHSSLRAFMM)

Perhaps the most dashing and romantic, however, was G. Charbonnaux, heir to the wealthy and famous family producing champagne of the same name. It was Charbonnaux who was behind the celebrations on Bastille Day 1943 when the squadron invited the local villagers and various dignitaries to a dinner on the base.

Rather more tragic was the story of Count Gabriel de Gramont, a talented French diplomat and heir to the Duke de Gramont. Gramont volunteered for the French Air Force as soon as war was declared in 1939, sending his family to live in Washington where he had served in the French Embassy. After the fall of France, de Gramont and a group of fellow officers stole a fishing boat and crossed the Channel to England. He spent the next three years flying missions in North Africa before returning to Britain to join the new No 342

Squadron. He was tragically killed on 10 April 1943 while learning to fly the new Boston aircraft. The cause of the crash was never firmly established, but the weather was foggy at the time.

On 10 April 1995 de Gramont's son, Georges travelled to West Raynham to join Vice Admiral Jean-Pierre Lucas, Colonel Bottine, Rev. Pere Coupet, local Mayor Raymond Nelson and the local Air Training Corps for a service of memorial and prayer. 'I am grateful that my father has been remembered,' said Georges de Gramont. 'For me it is a kind of reunion with my father. When he left to join de Gaulle I was only three.'

On 12 June 1944 No 342 Squadron began operations over northern France in the Boston aircraft supplied by the British. They invariably flew daylight raids at low level, most often against railway yards and other transportation targets. As D-Day approached, No 342 began to concentrate on the Calais area as part of the campaign to convince the Germans that the invasion would take place there, not in Normandy.

Members of the ground crew brave the elements to bomb-up a No 342 Squadron Boston in preparation for a mission in the spring of 1944.

On D-Day itself the squadron was sent to fly a series of shuttle missions along the coast near Ste Mere-Eglise, creating a curtain of smoke along the coast that covered the American troops landing on Utah Beach. The smoke bombs had to be delivered across a frontage of 10,000 yards, with one bomber dropping its load every 10 minutes. So successful was No 342 that they largely saved the assault troops from the heavy casualties the Americans took on neighbouring Omaha Beach. One aircraft was lost that day.

In October 1944 the squadron left West Raynham to take over a base in France, by which time it had left Bomber Command to become part of the 2nd Tactical Air Force.

Chapter 9

The Big 100

The summer of 1943 saw major changes for Bomber Command that would have a particular impact on Norfolk. The key event was the issuing of a new strategic directive by the Air Ministry to Air Chief Marshal Sir Arthur Harris on 10 June. This was codenamed Pointblank and was the result of months of sometimes tortuous negotiation between the US and British governments over war aims and how to achieve them.

Bomber Command's main objectives, Harris was told, were: 'The progressive destruction and dislocation of the German military, industrial and economic system, and the undermining of the morale of the German people to a point where their capacity for armed resistance is fatally weakened.' More detailed instructions told Harris to concentrate on German aircraft and U-boat manufacturing centres as the top priority, with oil, ball bearings, synthetic rubber and military vehicle factories being given secondary importance.

Harris was also told that he had to co-operate with the US 8th Air Force – 'the Mighty 8th', as the Americans called it. In theory the Americans would fly in daylight to bomb specified factories with deadly accuracy, after which the RAF would bomb the same area at night to destroy surrounding transport links and homes. In practice the Americans soon found that the Luftwaffe fighters were highly effective, and the German pilots equally skilled, at shooting down bombers operating in daylight. This aspect of Harris's new instructions would remain an objective only for some months to come.

Finally, Harris was told, preparations were underway to invade France at some unspecified place and time in the future. To prepare for this the government believed that the light and medium bombers of No 2 Group should be moved from Bomber Command to form a new 2nd Tactical Air Force. This would put the aircraft under the command of those planning the invasion and allow for a greater and more careful emphasis on targets that would prove useful to the invasion. Harris would be left with the strategic task of grinding down Germany.

Harris asked that he be allowed to keep Nos 105 and 139 Squadrons from No 2 Group, both flying out of Marham, within Bomber Command. He argued that these two Mosquito squadrons were in practice undertaking sorties more akin to those of the main bomber force than were the other squadrons of No 2 Group, equipped as they were with Bostons, Mitchells and Venturas. Harris, as he so often did, got what he asked for.

Another success for Harris was the creation of No 100 Group that followed that autumn. This secretive and highly specialised Group pulled together a

Wing Commander John Wooldridge points out some flak damage on his Mosquito to fellow aircrew of No 105 Squadron. Note the nose art to the right of the men. By the time this photo was taken No 105 was a specialist Pathfinder unit.

A No 199 Squadron crew briefing given by Wing Commander Bray. Operating out of North Creake, No 199 Squadron was one of the original members of the highly secretive No 100 Group. (www.feltwell.org)

variety of formations and technical innovations that were already in existence and allowed Harris to give high priority to their rapid improvement. The key task of No 100 Group was the defence of the main bomber force from German attacks.

The most established of the tactics to be employed by No 100 Group was the style of operation codenamed Intruder. These were attacks on Luftwaffe fighter and nightfighter bases, and on radar stations, aimed at knocking them out and so giving the bombers as easy a ride as possible. Intruder missions had been undertaken in a somewhat haphazard way since 1940, but since 1942 had been organised in a more planned fashion by Fighter Command using Nos 141, 169 and 239 Squadrons. These had been initially equipped with Beaufighters, but by late 1943 had Mosquitos. They were transferred to No 100 Group on 3 December.

The beautiful Tudor mansion of Blickling Hall was used as an officers' mess and guest quarters by No 100 Group. (Shaun Smith)

Window, the dropping of aluminium strips by decoy raiders, had already shown its effectiveness at producing false plots on German radar. Mandrel, a system based on ground stations in England, was able to jam German radar completely, but was only intermittently effective. Both made it difficult for the Germans to locate the incoming bomber stream accurately and so slowed the appearance of Luftwaffe nightfighters.

Bomber Command had also been experimenting with ways of distracting the nightfighters once they made contact with the bombers. The most imaginative of these was the inclusion in bomber formations of a Wellington packed with airborne radar and carrying a radio operator who spoke fluent German. These aircraft were able to pick up the nightfighters as they manoeuvred to attack, then listened in on the instructions coming from the ground based radar. The more successful radio operators were able not only to issue false instructions to the nightfighters, but even to mimic the voice and accent of the real German controller. Again, the results could be spectacularly successful, but the ploy did not always work.

Rather more daring was one of the first innovations to come out of No 100 Group itself: Serrate. This was the codename given to Mosquitos painted black and equipped with monitoring devices that could pick up German nightfighter radar pulses. The Mosquitos would then home in on the enemy aircraft and try to shoot it down. By the end of 1944 some three or four Serrate Mosquitos accompanied each major raid.

The most successful Serrate pilot proved to be Harold White of No 141 Squadron, who had already been awarded a DFC in September 1943. After moving to West Raynham, White flew a large number of Serrate missions with Michael Allen, DFC, as his navigator. By April they had shot down a confirmed five Luftwaffe nightfighters and had damaged, or possibly destroyed, eight more. On one sortie they engaged three enemy fighters in separate combats, for which they were awarded bars to their DFCs. In October the pair were awarded a second bar to their DFCs for a sortie the details of which were kept secret. They ended the war having shot down at least twelve enemy aircraft on Serrate missions.

The control tower and emergency room of RAF West Raynham of No 100 Group. This station was home to Nos 141 and 239 Squadrons, both flying Mosquitos, when the war ended. (Shaun Smith)

A service held on ANZAC Day 2006 at the memorial to Nos 462 and 464 Squadrons. Both these were Australian units that served in Norfolk. No 462 was part of No 100 Group and flew from Foulsham, while No 464 was a medium bomber squadron flying out of Feltwell. (John Blakeley)

For the rest of the war, No 100 Group was to fly missions of varying degrees of secrecy in efforts to protect their colleagues in the main bomber force. They would also continue to test and operate increasingly sophisticated electronics of varying degrees of effectiveness. Theirs was to be a crucial role in the Bomber Command effort.

The majority of the bomber bases in Norfolk were handed over to No 100 Group. West Raynham, Little Snoring, Swannington and Great Massingham had Mosquito squadrons while B-17 Fortresses flew out of Sculthorpe and Oulton. Oulton also had a Liberator squadron, while Foulsham was home to Wellingtons, Halifaxes and Mosquitos. The sole Stirling squadron, No 199, flew out of North Creake.

Marham was transferred to No 8 Group, the Pathfinders. It did not stay open for long, however, as in March 1944 it was closed down for a major reconstruction to turn it into a very heavy bomber base. It is still a major bomber base for jet aircraft of the RAF, but was to play no future role in the war as it did not reopen until 1946. Meanwhile Downham Market remained in service as a Pathfinder station with No 635 Squadron flying Lancasters.

Feltwell and Methwold were put into No 3 Group. Feltwell was used as a training base while Methwold was home to No 139 Squadron which had Stirlings in 1944, changing to Lancasters by 1945.

The various reorganisations were complete by the end of January 1944. The RAF in Norfolk had assumed the form that it would keep through to the end of the war.

Throughout the changes and reorganisations the normal business of Bomber Command continued unabated. No 218 Squadron continued to fly its Stirlings out of Downham Market on numerous raids. While on the way to raid Kassel, the Stirling flown by Sergeant John Riley was hit by a flak shell that knocked out one of the starboard engines. After a hurried conversation with the flight engineer, Riley decided to push on.

Over Kassel itself another flak shell struck the aircraft. This time all of the port wing beyond the second engine was blown away. The bomber lurched to port and went into a spinning dive. While he wrestled with the controls, Sergeant Riley ordered his crew to bale out. As soon as he got the Stirling back into level flight, the crew members leapt out one by one to float to earth by parachute. Left alone, Riley switched to autopilot and prepared to jump himself. As soon as he let go of the controls, the bomber lurched and began to dive. He took control again, getting the bomber level once more. When he again let go, the bomber lurched less violently so Riley scrambled to throw himself out of the hatch while he had the chance. By this time the bomber was very low and his parachute fall ended with him sustaining a broken hip.

One of the crew wrote home about his gallant conduct in keeping the aircraft level so that his colleagues could escape. In May 1944, Sergeant Riley received a letter in his prison camp telling him that he had been awarded a DFM.

On one of these raids to Hanover a swarm of wild sow nightfighters closed in to attack the bomber stream as it approached the target. The bomber flown by Canadian Flight Lieutenant Robert Cochrane was attacked by no fewer than three different fighters as it made its approach, but managed to escape damage. As it left the target, Cochrane's aircraft once again drew German attention when a Junkers Ju 88 nightfighter closed in. This time the upper gunner, Sergeant Kenneth Jones, managed to get an accurate seven second burst in on the enemy aircraft, which caught fire and went into a vertical dive.

Four nights later Flight Lieutenant Cochrane's crew had an even closer brush with German nightfighters. Over Mannheim a flak shell blew three feet off the end of the port wing, and peppered the rest of it with shrapnel holes. The Stirling's wing was none too large in any case, and the loss of the tip caused the aircraft to wallow badly and lose height. Nevertheless, Cochrane managed to get his aircraft and crew safely back home.

By this time Berlin was one of the targets most feared by the crews of the RAF. The Germans had set up powerful flak batteries around the city and placed several nightfighter bases close by. Bombing the capital of the Third Reich had the added danger that it was so far from Britain and involved a long flight over hostile territory. Nevertheless, it was a valuable target to which Harris sent his bombers on numerous occasions.

Pilot Officer Garth Hughes of No 514 Squadron, an Australian, was on his sixth trip to Berlin when his Lancaster was engaged by a nightfighter. Hughes corkscrewed his heavy bomber and managed to shake off the enemy. He was just congratulating himself on a job well done when a fire suddenly broke out in the cockpit, presumably having been started by the bullets of the attacker. Dense and choking, the smoke filled the cockpit so rapidly that Hughes could soon see neither his instruments nor anything outside the aircraft. The flight engineer scrambled to put out the fire with a small extinguisher.

At this critical moment the tail gunner reported another Luftwaffe fighter approaching. Relying entirely on the running commentary from the rear and upper gunners, Pilot Officer Hughes threw his Lancaster into a series of evasive moves while flying totally blind. Once the second attacker was shaken off, the fire was got under control. Although most instruments were by now useless and one engine had packed up, Hughes got his aircraft home with an uninjured crew.

Also returning alive from Berlin were the crew of Squadron Leader John Overton of No 218 Squadron. Overton's Stirling was attacked by a nightfighter as it approached Berlin. An engine was set on fire, while the tail gunner and wireless operator were wounded. The upper gunner fought back with determination, calmly talking Overton through the movements of the enemy so that he could take evasive action. After some five minutes of combat, the German was shot down. By this time Overton's aircraft was out of position and far below the main bomber stream. Despite the risk of attracting another Luftwaffe fighter, or of being hit by bombs falling from above, Overton pushed on to bomb Berlin before turning for home.

Another tough target was Schweinfurt, a town in southern Germany, home to a major ball-bearing factory that was crucial to the construction of Germany's much feared panzers. The American 8th Air Force twice tried to bomb the factory by day, but lost almost 20% of their aircraft and failed to destroy the target. Bomber Command were sent to see what they could do.

Pilot Officer James Hydes of No 514 Squadron took part in one raid on Schweinfurt. As the bomber stream approached the target, the aircraft in front of and above Hydes' was hit and suddenly exploded. A lump of burning debris crashed through the cockpit cover and landed at his feet. Moving quickly, Hydes snatched it up, but dropped it when it proved to be both heavier and hotter than he expected. He then grabbed an extinguisher and put it out before it could set light to the aircraft. The Schweinfurt raids proved to be ineffective, largely because the Germans had dispersed ball-bearing manufacture away from Schweinfurt after the first American raid.

A piece of flaming debris struck another No 514 Lancaster over Frankfurt. This time it fell through the upper turret, smashing the starboard perspex cover and coming to rest next to the turret's ammunition store. Realising that the flames could set off the hundreds of rounds of ammunition with deadly effect, the upper gunner, Flying Officer Harold Bryant, scrambled down from his sling seat, grabbed the blazing object in his gloved hands and heaved it out by the hole through which it had come. Bryant then climbed back into the turret. Despite the howling wind coming through the hole, and the fact that he had to hold his oxygen supply tube together with one hand while operating the guns with the other, he stayed at his post for the rest of the mission.

Like No 514, No 218 Squadron was to leave Norfolk in 1944. Before that it took part in several raids into occupied France. On one such raid the Stirling flown by Pilot Officer Ronald Scammell was attacked by two Luftwaffe fighters. In the ensuing battle the flight engineer was killed and all other crew members, except for Scammell himself, wounded. As the combat drew to a close, he had a close escape when a hail of bullets smashed his control panel to fragments. Reduced to flying without assistance, without any instruments and with the flaps not working, Scammell managed to get his bomber back to England. Once over an emergency landing strip he realised that the undercarriage was not working either. Unable to bale out without abandoning his wounded crew, he put his heavy bomber down into a crash-landing that tore the floor out of the fuselage. Fortunately no additional injuries were suffered in the impact.

In contrast, No 149 Squadron was to stay in the county, at Methwold, to the end of the war, first on Stirlings and later flying Lancasters. It was while they still flew Stirlings that rear gunner Sergeant Charles Wale spent his 28th sortie attacking Frankfurt. As the bomber approached the town it was attacked from behind by a pair of Junkers Ju 88 nightfighters. The first German made a half-hearted attack then dived off, but the second proved to be more tenacious. The Luftwaffe pilot closed the range to under 200 yards, at which point Wale let fly a five second burst which caused the enemy to burst into flames. Wale watched the burning aircraft as it dived to earth through more than two miles of sky and exploded on impact. When Wale completed his tour, his squadron commander wrote: 'Flight Sergeant Wale's devotion to duty has never waivered and his keenness and tenacity have always been of the highest order.'

On a mission to Bochum in May 1944 another gunner of No 149 Squadron was awarded an immediate DFM for his shooting. Sergeant William Aspey was on his 28th operation as rear gunner when a Ju 88 appeared, shadowing the Stirling from a distance. Aspey reported the German aircraft to his pilot and kept a careful watch on it. After some minutes, the Ju 88 came into the attack. Aspey and the upper gunner shot back. Three times the German attacked, without inflicting any damage, after which it broke off the combat. Over the target itself, a Focke Wulf Fw 190 came screaming down from above, firing wildly. It dived straight past and vanished into the darkness.

Handley Page Halifax

Type:	Heavy bomber
Engines:	Mk I - V 4 x 1280 hp
	Rolls-Royce Merlin X
	Mk VI - IX 4 x 1800 hp
	Bristol Hercules 100
Wingspan:	98 ft 10 in
Length:	70 ft 1 in
Height:	20 ft 9 in
Weight:	Empty 33,860 lb
	Loaded 65,000 lb
Armament:	Mk I-V 8 x 0.303 in machine guns in nose and tail turrets
	and beam windows
	Mk VI-IX 8 x 0.303 in machine guns in dorsal and tail turrets
	and ventral opening.
Bomb-load:	13,000 lb
Max speed:	265 mph
Ceiling:	18,000 ft (Mk I)
Range:	2,400 miles with reduced bomb-load
Production:	6,176

It was in 1937 that Handley Page began work on a four-engine bomber to replace the Hampden, which was then its main production bomber aircraft. The Halifax proved to be a dependable and versatile aircraft which flew with Coastal Command as well as Bomber Command. The roomy fuselage proved especially useful for variants, such as its role as a paratroop transport, electronic countermeasures and cargo aircraft.

The eventful night was still not over for Sergeant Aspey. As the bomber left the Bochum area another Ju 88 appeared. Without hesitating, the nightfighter closed in from behind and opened fire. Again Aspey shot back. In the two attacks it made, the Junkers inflicted only minor damage before vanishing into the night. Some time later, as the bomber approached the North Sea, a fourth fighter appeared. This Fw 190 came up from the rear.

Consolidated B-24 Liberator

Type:	Heavy bomber
Engines:	4 x 1200 hp Pratt & Whitney R-1830-43
Wingspan:	110 ft
Length:	66 ft 4 in
Height:	17 ft 11 in
Weight:	Empty 32,605 lb
	Loaded 71,200 lb
Armament:	10 x 0.5 in machine guns in dorsal, tail, nose and ventral positions
Bomb-load:	8,000 lb
Max speed:	303 mph
Ceiling:	32,000 ft
Range:	2,850 miles
Production:	18,482

American factories produced more Liberators than any other type of aircraft during the Second World War. Although it was designed as a bomber, the Liberator was also produced in transport, tanker and maritime patrol versions as it proved its worth in combat. The distinctively deep fuselage was mounted on a tricycle undercarriage, which was considered very advanced for a bomber when the Liberator was first produced in 1940. Of the squadrons flying out of Norfolk only No 223 Squadron at Oulton had this aircraft.

Aspey knew by now that he was running low on ammunition so he held his fire until the enemy was close, even though bullets were spattering around him. Aspey then let fly with a single burst which tore into the nose of the Fw 190, causing it to break up and fall from the sky.

While the squadrons in No 3 Group continued to play their role in the main bomber force, the Mosquito squadrons pushed ahead with their more specialist work. In December 1943 a pair of the fast bombers from No 105 squadron were sent to hit a factory in the Ruhr. They reached the target without difficulty but as the Mosquitos roared in to drop their bombs a flak shell exploded directly under the nose of the aircraft piloted by Flying Officer William Humphrey. The explosion sheared off the tip of the aircraft nose, damaged the controls and sent a sliver of metal to slice off part of Humphrey's flying boot and cut two of his toes. Nevertheless, the bombing run was completed successfully and Humphrey got his aircraft home, though he had to take some ribbing from comrades about his 'ventilated boot'.

Even as the men of Bomber Command in Norfolk were settling down after the extensive reorganisations to which they had been subjected, a new change was imposed. The long awaited invasion of occupied Europe that was to become famous as D-Day was almost at hand. Bomber Command was needed to smooth the way for the army.

Chapter 10

Overlord

RAF Feltwell seen from the air in the summer of 1944. There have been attempts made to camouflage the distinctive outlines of the control tower and hangars, while false field boundaries have been painted across the grass and runways.
(www.feltwell.org)

An aerial view of RAF Marham following its wartime rebuilding which saw the construction of three massive concrete runways, clearly visible in this picture.

By **May 1944** the planning for D-Day, the Allied invasion of occupied France, was complete. All that was needed was a spell of suitable weather and the great enterprise could be launched. The 2nd Tactical Air Force, formerly No 2 Group of Bomber Command, had been pounding targets in France for months. But with the invasion imminent, the main bomber force was required.

At first transport links right across northern France were the target. As many places outside as inside the invasion area of Normandy were hit so as to confuse the Germans about where the invasion would take place. The plan was to disrupt the flow of enemy reinforcements and supplies to the area. As the date grew nearer the bombing raids shifted to airfields, coastal batteries and other, smaller targets. Harris was not happy with this as his

141

Aircrew of No 199 Squadron prepare for debriefing after a mission carried out in the run up to D-Day. (www.feltwell.org)

men were not trained to hit such small targets – and the results often bore out his views.

Meanwhile No 100 Group was getting ready for some very specialist work. The Stirlings of Nos 214 and 199 Squadrons were converted from bombers to become mobile radar jamming units using the Mandrel device. Other squadrons were put to work practising precision manoeuvres or getting accustomed to new and often bizarre equipment.

On 5 June the final orders were given that the invasion would take place next day. The regular bombing squadrons of No 3 Group in Norfolk took off to attack targets in and around Normandy, while No 100 Group began its specialist work. First into the air, around dusk, were Nos 199 and 214 Squadrons. The aircraft of No 199 took up station at 15,000 feet along the south coast of England, from Dorset to Dover. Flying at precisely determined intervals, heights and bearings, the aircraft jammed German radar across the entire central and eastern English Channel, masking the invasion fleet.

Meanwhile, No 214 Squadron was heading east to fly over Calais and along the Somme valley depositing specially designed Window. This set up a false echo on the German radar sets that simulated a mass of bomber aircraft heading for precisely those targets that would be chosen if the invasion were about to take place near Calais. To further this illusion the Serrate anti-nightfighter Mosquitos of Nos 141, 160 and 239 Squadrons were present over the Somme, attacking any nightfighters they could locate. Simultaneously Nos 85, 157 and 515 Squadrons attacked Luftwaffe bases as far east as Holland, again to give the impression that Calais, not Normandy, was the invasion target.

This was so successful at diverting German defences that in July Nos 192

A Boston drops bombs on German positions on D-Day. The black and white 'invasion stripes' were painted on all Allied aircraft taking part in the campaign to enable fellow pilots and ground-based anti-aircraft gunners to recognise friend from foe with speed and accuracy.

and 199 Squadrons were converted into the so-called Special Window Force (SWF) within No 100 Group. Their mission was to channel attention away from the main bomber force by pretending to be a second major force raiding a quite different target. The crews referred to the task as 'spoofing'.

Going into action around midnight, No 149 Squadron had the task of dropping 'Ruperts'. These half-sized dummy parachutists were armed with fireworks which went off when the dummy landed to simulate machine gun fire. They were dropped at various locations to confuse the German defenders as to where the real parachute troops were landing and proved to be most successful.

The dangerous, yet secretive nature of much of what No 100 Group was doing at this time is reflected in the award of medals. On 27 June, Sergeant Harvey Allin of No 192 Squadron was awarded a DFM for unspecified acts of 'cool courage and ardour whilst engaged on special duties'.

Once D-Day was over, Bomber Command reverted to attacking communications and transport targets in northern France and the Low Countries. Germany was not ignored, however. Harris argued rightly that if he abandoned all attacks on Germany during this period, the enemy would shift their nightfighters to France. He therefore raided several targets in Germany, albeit at infrequent intervals, to keep the defences dispersed and so relatively ineffective.

Among the tasks that were generally reckoned to be the least dangerous were the 'Gardening' missions – laying mines in the shipping routes between Germany and ports in occupied areas of Scandinavia and around the Baltic. Such missions could, however, be extremely hazardous when the task was to mine approaches to heavily defended ports. In June a force of No 149 Squadron was sent to mine the waters off Kiel. So close to the port did Pilot Officer William Holmes bring down his aircraft that he was picked up by searchlights on the harbour and came under fire from flak guns. The lights blinded the bomb-aimer, who was unable to drop the mines. Again the bomber came in, and again the searchlights made mining impossible. Not until the third pass could the mines be dropped, by which time the bomber was riddled by shrapnel.

By this date the Germans had realised that the first aircraft over a target were the Pathfinders, dropping flares and markers for the main bomber stream to use as aiming points. The Luftwaffe fighters made particular attempts to attack these aircraft, not only in the hope of destroying them but also to try to upset their aim and so disrupt the bombing of those following.

A view from inside the rear turret of a Lancaster looking out. Tail gunners sat in this perch for long hours on missions, constantly aware of the need to remain absolutely vigilant in case of enemy attack.

Aircraft using Oboe – and its various derivatives such as Pepperbox, Penwiper and Fountain Pen – to get an accurate fix on their position were especially vulnerable as they had to fly straight and level for some minutes for the electronic system to communicate with base stations in Britain and compute the position.

On a raid on the naval and merchant dockyards at Friedrichshafen a Lancaster of No 635 Squadron was acting as lead Pathfinder. It therefore found itself attacked by two Junkers Ju 88s and Focke Wulf Fw 190 as it made its approach run. The rear gunner, Sergeant Robert Edie from Canada, opened fire and rather surprised himself when one German aircraft dived away damaged, a second exploded in a ball of flame and the third veered sharply off to avoid a similar fate. The upper gunner had not even had time to get his guns to bear.

Another No 635 Pathfinder, piloted by Squadron Leader Harry Johnston, was less fortunate when it flew to mark the railway marshalling yards at Nantes on the night of 11 June. Because the yards were close to the city centre, accurate marking was needed if French civilian casualties were to be avoided. The target was covered by a thick blanket of cloud, so Johnston dived down to 2,000 feet to get a clear view. As the aircraft circled it was picked up by a searchlight, and almost at once hit by a light flak battery. Tail gunner Sergeant John Ledgerwood fired back and put out the searchlight, causing the flak to cease fire. He then turned around to see that the fuselage of the aircraft was a blazing mass of tangled metal struts immediately behind his turret. Almost simultaneously, Ledgerwood heard the pilot's command over the intercom to abandon the aircraft. He found that his parachute had

Gladys Robinson (above) was a driver attached to Great Massingham in 1944 whose main task was to drive and maintain supply lorries (opposite).
(Massingham MHSSLRAFMM)

been burned in the fire and hurriedly reported that he could not bale out.

By this time most of the crew had already jumped. Squadron Leader Johnston told Sergeant Ledgerwood to try to put the fire out and then join him and wireless operator Roland Padden in the cockpit. The emergency fire extinguisher doused the flames, but failed to put the fire out completely. Ledgerwood then turned to his 'Mae West' lifejacket and parachute harness to beat at the remaining flames. He was working his way forwards through the fuselage to deal with the last glowing embers when there was a sickening sound of tearing metal, the Lancaster gave a sudden lurch forward and he was swept by an icy cold blast of air. Looking round he saw that the rear turret where he had been sitting had fallen off, taking a section of fuselage with it.

The howling wind coming in through the gaping hole in the rear of the aircraft put out the last vestiges of the fire, so Sergeant Ledgerwood scrambled forward. His face, arms and hands had been badly burned while fighting the fire in the confined space of the fuselage, and he could not see out of one eye. Despite these injuries he promptly reported to Squadron Leader Johnston. Refusing to lie down and be treated by Padden, Ledgerwood scrambled into the still functioning upper turret and remained there, alert for enemy fighters, until the wounded aircraft staggered back to England to crash-land at the first airfield it reached.

On 13 June a new phase in the air war opened when the Germans launched the first V1 against Britain. Officially known as the *Vergeltungswaffe*, or Revenge Weapon, the V1 was quickly dubbed the Doodlebug by the British due to its distinctive engine noise. It was essentially a pilotless aircraft powered by a ram jet engine that covered a powerful explosive warhead. Before launch, the course of the V1 was set by a gyroscopic compass device and the range predetermined by the amount of fuel in the tank. The weapon had a range of 160 miles and a warhead of 1,870 lb. This put London well within its reach and made it able to do considerable damage to property and people.

The British government was deeply worried about the material damage that the V1 could inflict, and also by the impact the eerie weapon might have on public morale. Bomber Command was ordered to attack the launch sites and the storage depots where they were stored.

One such raid was a daylight attack on the storage depot at Trossy St Maxim on 3 August. Flying a No 635 Squadron Lancaster as a Pathfinder out of Downham Market was Squadron Leader Ian Bazalgette, a Canadian brought up in England. Bazalgette was a veteran of Bomber Command in Norfolk, having completed his first tour with No 115 Squadron at East Wretham. He had won a DFC on that tour, then spent some months training new air crew before returning to operations with No 635 in April 1944. For the raid on 3 August, he had his regular crew, with the exception of the upper gunner who was ill and whose place was taken by an Australian, Sergeant V.V. Leeder.

As the formation of Lancasters came within sight of Trossy St Maxim, a pair of Mosquitos raced across the site at low level, dropping precision markers. Squadron Leader Bazalgette's task was to drop colour-coded markers bracketing the precision markers for the guidance of the massed bombers coming immediately behind him. As he approached the target a massively powerful barrage of flak came up. His aircraft was hit three times in less than ten seconds and the fuselage caught fire. The bomb aimer, Flight Lieutenant I. Hibberd was seriously wounded by shrapnel and had to be given morphine. The upper gunner, Sergeant Leeder, was choked by the smoke and fumes, falling unconscious. Another hit knocked out both starboard engines and riddled the wing with holes.

Despite the carnage, Squadron Leader Bazalgette dropped his marker accurately, then his aircraft dropped its starboard wing and began to spin down. He wrestled control back again and ordered the crew to bale out. Cameron, the rear gunner, left his turret to come forward but found himself ankle deep in petrol that was sloshing about in the rear of the fuselage. He baled out, as did the other members of the crew able to do so. Turner, the flight engineer, tried to argue with Bazalgette, but was given a direct order to take to his parachute. He left behind Bazalgette, Sergeant Leeder and the badly wounded Flight Lieutenant Hibberd.

By the time Turner left the doomed aircraft it was wallowing along at barely a thousand feet. As he landed he saw the bomber coming down with its undercarriage up in an open field close to what turned out to be the village of Senantes. The bomber made a perfect belly landing, sliding across the ground to come to a gentle halt. But before any of the three men inside could clamber out the leaking petrol caught alight and the aircraft exploded in a ball of flame. All three were killed.

The four surviving crew members were taken in by the French Resistance and hidden for several months until the advancing Allied armies liberated the area. They then presented themselves to an army officer and were taken back to Britain for a rest and then a return to duty. When they told their

A squadron planning room. Once ordered by Group to prepare for a sortie it was down to the squadron commander to decide which aircraft and crews would be flying that night.

story, which was confirmed by the French locals who had witnessed the mighty Lancaster landing and exploding, Squadron Leader Bazalgette was awarded a posthumous Victoria Cross.

The courage and devotion to each other shown by the crew, and in particular by Squadron Leader Bazalgette who could easily have saved himself, was typical of Bomber Command crews. Most men preferred to fly with comrades that they knew and trusted. Crews that formed at Operational Training Units tended to stay together, barring sickness or injury, throughout their tour of duty. However, some men had skills so highly prized that they were requested by pilots for particular missions.

One such man was Sergeant Herbert Bailey of No 149 Squadron. Bailey was a flight engineer of great skill and dedication, but his main talent was his complete coolness. No matter what mayhem or carnage might be breaking out around him, Bailey sat quietly monitoring his dials and controls as if he were sitting in a quiet office somewhere in England. By this date the job of a flight engineer was indeed complex and demanding. It was the flight engineer who monitored all the instruments connected to the four engines, keeping an eye out for overheating or other problems, and who watched for icing, altitude and other measurements. Remaining always alert, the flight engineer had to take action to correct any faults. This task was especially important when the aircraft was damaged.

Sergeant Bailey was credited with saving his aircraft at least twice. On the first occasion two Luftwaffe nightfighters shot up the fuselage, forcing Bailey to make running repairs to many instruments while the aircraft corkscrewed around the sky taking evasive manoeuvres. On the second, his Stirling was badly hit by flak. One starboard engine caught fire and the other was damaged. Working with his trademark calm and coolness, Bailey first extinguished the fire, then spent the next four hours nursing the damaged engine as it threatened to overheat or lose pressure. By carefully regulating the revs and oil flow, Bailey kept the engine working all the way home. At the end of his tour, he was awarded a DFM. 'Flight Sergeant Bailey,' the citation read, 'has flown with no less than nine different pilots, all of whom speak of his exceptional abilities with the highest praise. He has at all times shown himself to be a keen and resourceful Flight Engineer.' No 149 Squadron missed him badly when he left operational duties to train new engineers.

Another exceptional man was tail gunner Sergeant Cyril Green who completed his second tour with No 635 Squadron at Downham Market. His already impressive reputation was cemented on a raid over Germany in August when he spotted a Luftwaffe twin-engine nightfighter creeping up on a fellow Lancaster of No 635 from behind and below. Realising that the crew of the other bomber had not seen their danger, Green asked his own pilot to drop altitude slightly to give him a better aim at the enemy nightfighter. Then, with a prolonged burst of fire from his four machine guns, Green calmly shot the German out of the sky.

A second highly rated rear gunner was Vince Jamieson, a New Zealander in 149 Squadron. On a raid to Berlin just before the D-Day campaign opened, Jamieson shot down two German fighters in quick succession.

By the end of August 1944 most of the storage depots and identified launch sites for the V1 had been destroyed. The Germans switched to mobile launchers and smaller depots to keep up the momentum of the 'V' weapon campaign. They also introduced the deadly V2, a rocket that flew faster than the speed of sound and against which there was no air defence. Dangerous though these weapons remained, they did not constitute large enough targets for heavy bombers to be effective against them. Harris was ordered to return his main force to the attack on Germany. By now it was known that Germany was critically short of fuel, so raids on oil installations and oil supply routes were given top priority.

Bomber Command was going back to Germany.

Junkers Ju 88C

Type:	Night fighter
Engines:	2 x 1400 hp Junkers Jumo 211JB
Wingspan:	65 ft 10 in
Length:	47 ft 1 in
Height:	16 ft 7 in
Weight:	Empty 18,871 lb
	Loaded 27,226 lb
Armament:	3 x 20 mm cannon
	and 3 x 7.92 mm machine guns in nose,
	plus 1 x 13 mm machine gun in rear cockpit
	plus 2 x 20 mm cannon firing upward
Max speed:	311 mph
Ceiling:	32,000 ft
Range:	1,230 miles
Production:	3,200

The Junkers Ju 88 was designed as a high-speed medium bomber in 1936, but in 1939 the addition of more powerful engines made a fighter-bomber version possible. With the increasing impact of RAF Bomber Command's campaign against Germany, a further modification led to the development of the Ju 88C nightfighter variant. The bomb bay was removed and its place taken up by airborne radar which enabled the third crew member to direct the pilot to the bombers. In early 1944 production of the Ju 88C was halted in favour of the new Ju 88G, which had a completely redesigned fuselage housing more sophisticated radar and electronic countermeasures as well as improved weaponry. This aircraft accounted for more RAF bombers than all other models of Luftwaffe fighters combined.

Chapter 11

Back to Germany

By the time Sir Arthur Harris sent his main force of bombers back to Germany after the D-Day campaign, things had changed. The photographs brought back by high-flying Mosquitos were providing the 'boffins' with unparalleled details of potential targets. And the top secret 'Ultra' code-breaking station at Bletchley Park in Buckinghamshire was giving much vital information.

It was soon clear that the Bomber Command campaign of area bombing German industrial cities was proving to be horribly effective at reducing armaments output. There were still industrial centres that offered viable targets for area bombing, but there were now two new priorities. The first was oil, for the Third Reich had lost control of the oilfields of southern Russia and was desperately short of fuel. Oil supply facilities had been a priority target for Bomber Command before, but the small targets involved had been difficult to hit at night.

That particular problem had not changed by 1944, which was why a force of Halifaxes of No 463 Squadron left Foulsham on 6 October to bomb the oil plant of Sterkrade in daylight. On his 18th sortie was Sergeant Cecil Baldwin, the bomb-aimer. On the immediate approach to the target, the aircraft was hit by a flak shell that started a major fire. The pilot, Flying Officer Edward McGindle, ordered the crew to bale out, but as the third man dropped clear a second flak shell hit the aircraft, wounding Baldwin

The interior of the Air Traffic Control room at RAF Feltwell. By this stage in the war, the increasing prevalence of sophisticated electronics made the task of air traffic control one of the more complex on an air base. (www.feltwell.org)

slightly and the navigator more seriously.

Sergeant Baldwin reported to Flying Officer McGindle that the navigator was too badly wounded to use his parachute, then turned to bind the man's wounds. The pilot decided to try to reach Norfolk in the damaged aircraft. He turned away to the west, ordering the wireless operator, Sergeant Edward Whelan, to tackle the fire. Baldwin, who had had some elementary training as a navigator, took over the wounded man's station and navigated the aircraft back across the North Sea to England.

The flight engineer, Sergeant Stuart Soames, had meanwhile been trying to keep the damaged port inner engine going, but eventually gave up the struggle and switched it off. He walked to the rear of the aircraft to inspect the damage, reporting back that the tail control surfaces were badly shot about and most of the fuselage skin burnt away. He then nursed the wounded man for the rest of the trip. It was not until the aircraft crossed the coast that Sergeant Baldwin told Soames that he had been wounded, by which time he had lost so much blood that he passed out. Flying Officer McGindle managed to put the damaged bomber down safely at his home base.

Another oil target bombed in daylight was the refinery at Gelsenkirchen, attacked by No 462 Squadron on 12 September. The bomb-aimer on one of the Halifaxes was Sergeant John Gibson, who was on the 30th and final flight of his first tour of duty. The bombers had been promised partial cloud cover over the target, but they found the sky bereft of any cloud when they arrived. Naked and open to the defences though they were, the squadron went in on their bombing run. A flak shell exploded beneath Gibson's aircraft, shattering the canopy through which he was peering to aim the bombs. Shards of perspex peppered his face, blinding him with blood and debris. Despite this, Gibson calmly kept counting down to the moment of release. Although unable to see what he was doing, he managed to release his bombs on cue and alongside the other aircraft so that they must have landed close to if not on the target. His calm counting when in great pain

By the time Bomber Command returned to raids over Germany in strength, the Handley Page Halifax was second only to the Lancaster in importance as a heavy bomber.

A photograph taken during a low level raid by Mosquitos on armaments factories at Essen. An aircraft can be seen to the left of centre banking away after dropping its bombs.

was so effective that the rest of the crew did not realise anything was wrong until Gibson called them on the intercom to report that he would appreciate a bit of help.

The second priority target was a result of Bomber Command's own success. With so many factories bombed out, the Germans had moved production of some key components away from the larger cities to isolated rural settings, which made them very difficult to locate and bomb. But this dispersal of factories did mean that the various components now had to be moved around Germany a lot more than previously, so transportation links became increasingly important to the German war effort – and therefore an increasingly important target for Harris and his men.

Unfortunately, railways and canals were not only very thin targets to try to hit, but they could be easily repaired. Bridges and viaducts offered better

Wing Commander Reginald Reynolds (left) and Squadron Leader Edward Sismore pose beside their Mosquito on return from a raid on Jena in October 1944 for which both were awarded the DFC.

prospects as they might take some weeks to replace, but again were tricky targets to hit. Barnes Wallis, the inventive genius who had created both the Wellington bomber and the bouncing bomb that had destroyed the Ruhr dams in 1943, went to work to try to develop a weapon that could crack these targets. His creation was known officially as Tallboy, but was soon dubbed 'the earthquake bomb' by the press.

This Tallboy was an awesome weapon. It was 21 feet long and had a tip of specially hardened steel behind which the casing was as slender and streamlined as possible. When dropped from a great height, the bomb was able to bore down underground before exploding. The resulting blast lifted the ground surface up, like an earthquake, and undermined the foundations of any structures nearby. It was to prove highly effective against bridges, embankments and viaducts.

Tallboy was completed in July 1944, but at first it was present in very small

Pilot Roy Ralston (left) and navigator Syd Clayton stand beside their No 105 Squadron Mosquito in 1944.

numbers and could be used only against the highest priority targets. Thus it was that No 571 Squadron found itself detailed to attack the Dortmund-Ems Canal with the comparatively old-fashioned mines that had been used in the North Sea since the start of the war. Mines had to be dropped from a height of only 300 feet if they were not to be destroyed when they hit the water, while the long thin nature of a canal meant that the only way to be certain of dropping the mines in the water was to fly along its straight length. The Germans, of course, knew this and ensured that such stretches were heavily defended by light flak and searchlights.

The raid by No 571, led and planned in great detail by Wing Commander James Birkin, took place on a brilliant night of the full moon. This moonlight, it was hoped, would sparkle off the water of the canal and make it easy to spot, allowing the bombers to remain over the dangerous target area for as short a time as possible. Unfortunately when the bombers arrived a dense layer of cloud covered the whole area. Using Oboe, the lead aircraft dropped marking flares by parachute over the spot where the canal lurked beneath the cloud. One by one, the bombing Lancasters then had to drop down through the cloud, emerging into the full glare of searchlights and flak to race along the canal and drop their mines. Despite these difficulties, the raid was carried out with great precision in the face of heavy defensive fire. The survivors were awarded between them one DSO, five DFCs and a DFM, making this one of the most highly decorated raids of the war relative to the number of men involved.

The Mosquitos of No 464 Squadron were often despatched to harry German transport at night. On one sortie Sergeant John Carter was sent out to bomb a railway bridge north of the Ruhr. He not only successfully damaged the bridge, but found a train on the railway line which he subjected to a hail of gunfire. Unfortunately for Carter, a light flak gun was located by the bridge, and a shell hit his starboard engine and tore it from its mountings. The wooden Mosquito was not really designed to survive such treatment, but nevertheless Carter managed to nurse his wounded aircraft home to Sculthorpe.

General Curtiss Le May, head of the US 8th Air Force, takes the salute at a parade held at RAF Feltwell in 1944. He was visiting to present a medal to Cliff Rusted, who had rescued some US aircrew from an aircraft that crashed nearby. (www.feltwell.org)

By 1944 RAF Feltwell was a training station where aircrew were schooled in the art of flying Lancasters before being posted to an operational squadron. This photo shows the crew headed by Flight Lieutenant David Lyon during their time at Feltwell. (www.feltwell.org)

Meanwhile the area bombing raids on industrial cities continued. Brunswick was one of the first to be hit after the D-Day campaign, being raided on 12 August. Flying Halifaxes out of Foulsham, No 192 Squadron took part. As his bomber left the target, upper gunner Sergeant Leonard Dagnell was startled when his turret exploded in a shower of fragments, with blinding flashes of fire erupting where Luftwaffe machine-gun bullets struck the guns and metal fixtures. The sudden hail of destruction was over as quickly as it began – and Dagnell was miraculously unwounded. The turret was, however, smashed to pieces and the guns were jammed. Although this meant that Dagnell was sitting in the icy blast of a 200mph wind, he stayed in his turret to keep an eye open for any other German nightfighters that might be about. He was there, suffering agonies of cold and a touch of frostbite, until the Halifax reached English skies.

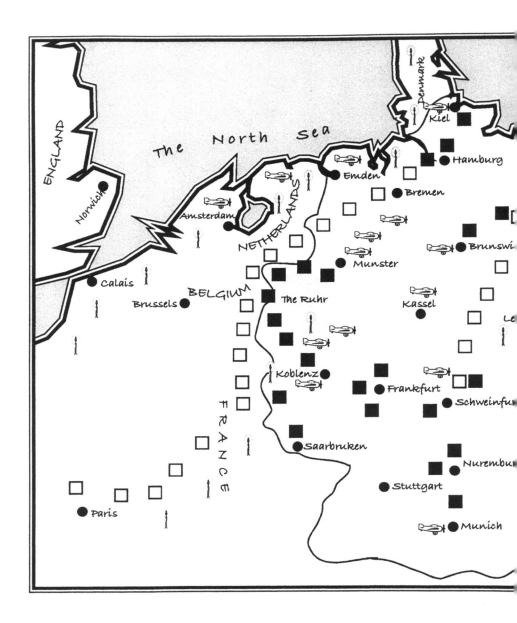

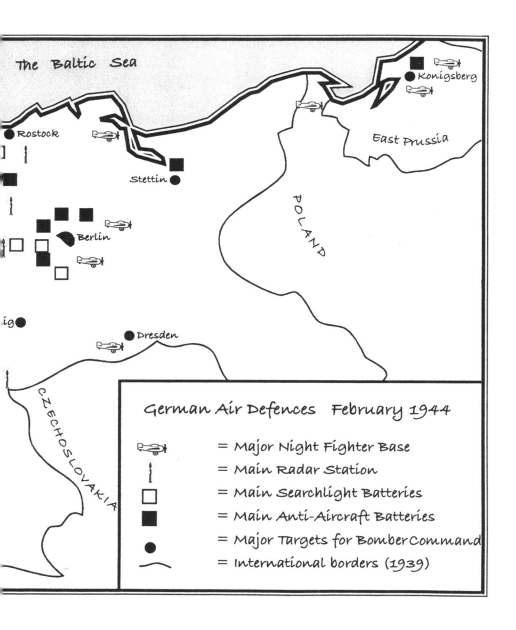

The Baltic Sea

Königsberg

East Prussia

Rostock

Stettin

POLAND

Berlin

ig

Dresden

CZECHOSLOVAKIA

German Air Defences February 1944

= Major Night Fighter Base
= Main Radar Station
= Main Searchlight Batteries
= Main Anti-Aircraft Batteries
= Major Targets for Bomber Command
= International borders (1939)

163

A bomb aimer peers through his sights while holding the bomb release button in his left hand. The need to take account of wind speed and direction made aiming bombs a tricky task throughout the war.

It was the opposite of frostbite that worried Sergeant Thomas Smith of No 149 Squadron on a raid in September, recorded only as being 'special operations'. Over Germany the aircraft was hit by flak which ruptured a fuel line, causing petrol to pour into the fuselage. The smallest spark would have set off a fire and explosion that would have killed all on board. Smith, the wireless operator, was ordered to open the rear door and try to bale the petrol out.

As he was busily engaged in this hazardous task, Sergeant Smith saw the flight engineer suddenly stand up and appear to dance a jig. Scrambling forwards, he found the flight engineer had been overcome by the fumes and was randomly throwing switches and turning dials on his controls, causing the engines and hydraulics to splutter and go into fits. There followed a bizarre and terrifying fight between Sergeant Smith and his delirious colleague. He tried to drag the man away from the control panel, while the flight engineer fought back with tenacity and all the time both men were ankle deep in petrol and choking on the fumes. The flight engineer eventually collapsed, allowing Smith to take over the controls. Although his training had been basic at best, he managed to reconnect the fuel supply to the engines and get the hydraulics working again. The stricken bomber got back to England, but caught fire as it landed. Sergeant Smith got out alive, but injured. After some time in hospital he returned to his squadron to finish the final three flights of his second tour.

A rather unexpected, but spectacular, problem affected Squadron Leader Bernard MacDermott of No 462 Squadron and his crew when sent to bomb the railway sidings of Acheres. Shortly after take-off from Foulsham, the rear gunner noticed that there was a small hole in the port tail fin of the Halifax. He reported it to the pilot, but the problem did not seem to be too serious so MacDermott opted to continue towards the target.

Bomber air crew pile onto a truck at dusk to be taken to their aircraft ready for a sortie.

Bomber's Moon. A lone RAF bomber drones through the night sky heading for Germany.

As the mission progressed, however, the hole appeared to be getting larger. The tail fin began to vibrate in the slipstream and by the time Acheres was reached, Squadron Leader MacDermott was having some problems getting the aircraft to fly straight. The vibrations and control problems got progressively worse as the Halifax headed home, with the rear gunner keeping up an increasingly worried commentary on the way that the hole was growing, sending fractures across the surface of the tail. As the bomber crossed the

'Tail-End Charlie' – a rear gunner prepares for action before take-off for Germany.

English coast, the vibrations suddenly got much worse. MacDermott decided that the safest option would be to have his crew bale out. Once the last man had gone, he engaged the autopilot and threw himself out. After dropping a short distance, he opened his parachute. He looked up to watch his aircraft drone away towards the sea. Suddenly the bomber seemed to fold in two just in front of the tail. Then it broke up completely with the forward part of the heavy aircraft falling towards the ground surrounded by a shower of fragments and pieces.

Whatever had caused that small hole had clearly been a very serious fault. Squadron Leader MacDermott and his crew had a very close escape.

The Lancaster flown by Flight Lieutenant Peter Mellor of No 635 Squadron to mark a target at Bochum in November proved to be rather more robust. On the flight out from Downham Market the Lancaster was coned by searchlights and hit several times by flak before it managed to escape back into the safety of the darkness. The port outer engine was knocked out, but Mellor decided to carry on regardless. Just as he turned for home after marking the target, the starboard inner engine failed.

Deciding to head for one of the emergency landing strips set up behind the lines of the advancing Allied forces in France, Flight Lieutenant Mellor headed west. The Lancaster was steadily losing height, but reached the landing ground safely. It was only when the undercarriage was lowered that Mellor realised that the port landing gear had been savagely damaged by flak and the tyres punctured. He nevertheless managed to land safely, allowing his entire crew to walk away uninjured.

While the heavy bombers were doing their jobs, the Mosquitos were continuing to fly Intruder missions to attack enemy fighter airfields, and those equipped with Serrate shadowed the main bomber streams to attack Luftwaffe nightfighters in the air. The airfield of Swannington had become operational only in May 1944 and was to be home to Nos 85 and 157 Squadrons. The most successful crew at this base proved to be the No 85 Mosquito team with Flight Lieutenant Bransome Burbridge as pilot and Flight Lieutenant Frank Skelton as his observer. In the course of their first tour of duty, Burbridge and Skelton shot down a confirmed seven enemy fighters with several others listed as damaged. They also managed to be awarded a DFC each, and then were both awarded a bar when the tour ended because 'they have displayed outstanding keenness, great skill and gallantry, setting an example worthy of the highest praise.'

Chapter 12

Towards the Final Victory

The year **1945 opened** with Bomber Command trying to get over a serious and ill-tempered disagreement between Sir Arthur Harris, Commander-in-Chief, and Sir Charles Portal, Chief of the Air Staff. Although the extent of the row was not known lower down the chain of command – and certainly not to the men flying out of Norfolk – it was to influence the types of sorties undertaken for the rest of the war.

The heart of the problem was that Portal was in possession of vitally important information that he was not allowed to give to Harris. This meant that Harris, not knowing all the facts, relied on the information that he did have. Portal gave orders based on what he knew, Harris argued against them using perfectly logical arguments based on what *he* knew.

For most of 1944 the Allies had been able to intercept and decode the majority of the military and government radio messages sent by German army units in the field. This showed that the enemy's war effort was being severely hampered by a lack of fuel. British government intelligence experts did some calculations and soon realised that the German armed forces would run out of fuel within twelve months, and even sooner if oil storage and refinery plants could be hit by Bomber Command. The problem was that this was all so highly secretive that even the people decoding the messages were not told what they were doing. There were probably only about 25 people who knew what was going on. If the Germans had realised that their

No RAF unit could function properly without its specialist support staff. Seen here are the radar engineers who kept the top secret air-to-air radar of No 169 Squadron's Mosquitos working, photographed in the spring of 1945.

supposedly unbreakable codes had been cracked, they would have changed them at once and the Allies would have been deprived of enormously valuable information.

Portal knew about the codebreaking – codenamed Ultra – and therefore knew that the targeting of oil was both vital and necessary. Harris did not know about the source of this information and was baffled by Portal's insistence. Harris remembered earlier directives telling him that if only ball-bearings or molybdenum or rubber could be denied to the Germans, then the enemy war production would grind to a halt. Time and again, Harris had sent bomber crews on extremely dangerous missions to hit these supposedly invaluable targets. Many crews had been killed, but although the targets had been bombed the Germans did not seem to suffer the severe blow Harris had been promised.

Now Harris was being asked to do it again. He did not want to risk his men unnecessarily. He knew that the area bombing of industrial centres was having an effect, as were attacks on transport links. Harris preferred

An aerial photograph of RAF Massingham taken a few weeks after the end of the war. The triangle of runways is clearly visible near the centre of the photo as are the 'spectacles' where bombers were parked for dispersal around the perimeter. The village of Great Massingham lies at the bottom right. (Massingham MHSSLRAFMM)

By the end of the war the central areas of many German cities were vast piles of rubble with barely a building left intact. This is Cologne in September 1945.

to keep his men bombing targets of known worth rather than shift them to dangerous targets of doubtful importance.

In any case, Harris argued forcibly, the US 8th Air Force was better equipped and trained for precision bombing. Now that long range day fighters could escort the Flying Fortresses all the way over Germany such raids were no longer as costly as before. The RAF Bomber Command was better suited to area bombing, be it of industrial centres or transport links.

So serious did the conflict between the two become that Portal and Harris stopped talking and instead wrote each other formal letters. In the last two months of 1944 they wrote 24 letters, totalling 25,000 words on the subject. In the end, Harris offered to resign but Portal refused the offer. The dispute was never really resolved, but for the immediate future it was masked by the dreadful winter weather over Europe, which made precision attacks on small oil targets impracticable anyway.

In early February 1945 the Allied army commanders asked if Harris could bomb two towns close to the front line that the Germans were known to

The imposing statue of Air Chief Marshal Sir Arthur Harris, Commander-in-Chief of Bomber Command, that stands outside St Clement Danes church in London. After the war he became Managing Director of the South Africa Marine Corporation, retiring in 1953 and dying in 1984.

have fortified heavily: Kleve and Goch. The Allied ground advance into Germany was aiming to go through these two towns, and it was hoped that an air attack first would reduce casualties. The raid was carried out on 7 February and proved to be a turning point. Kleve in particular was reduced to rubble and utter destruction. When the Allied armies advanced they found that they were held up more by the rubble created by the bombing than by the surviving German troops.

Bomber Command now undoubtedly had the ability to reach targets and bomb them accurately – and it could deliver a heavy enough bomb-load to destroy them. Railway viaducts fell before the growing might of the bombers, as did naval bases, U-boat shelters and transportation centres. Germany was being gradually strangled, as the ground armies closed in from both east and west.

That is not to say that the Germans had given up. Far from it. Even as defeat loomed for the Third Reich new and deadlier weapons were being introduced. The autumn of 1944 saw the combat debut of two revolutionary German fighter aircraft, but it was in the early months of 1945 that they entered the war in numbers.

The first to enter service, in July 1944, was the Messerschmitt Me 262

The Messerschmitt Me 262 jet fighter.

Schwalbe, or Swallow. Allied airmen were astonished by the aircraft's top speed of 540 mph and feared its powerful armament of four 30 mm cannon in the nose. But what really amazed Allied flyers was that the Me 262 had no propellers: it was the first jet fighter to enter service anywhere in the world. The Me 262 was virtually impossible for air gunners to hit as it flew too fast and before long it began to take a heavy toll on bombers. Fortunately for the Allies, problems with production meant that only 200 of these superb aircraft ever entered service.

One of the first RAF men to see an Me 262 in action and survive to give a clear account of the encounter was Sergeant Charles Rees, rear gunner in a No 462 Squadron Lancaster over Berlin in November 1944. The bomber was leaving the target area, having dropped its bombs, when Rees saw the ominous shape of a small aircraft approaching from behind. The size of the stranger showed it was a single-seat fighter, which meant it could only be a German. Rees swung his turret round to bear and prepared to open fire, but was taken by surprise by the sheer speed with which the enemy fighter approached. Fortunately the Messerschmitt missed the bomber with its cannon, but Rees saw it going around for a second attack.

This time Sergeant Rees was determined not to be caught out by the unfamiliar attacker. He fired his guns, aiming well ahead of where the aircraft was in the hope of getting his bullets to fall where the Messerschmitt would be by the time it got there. Rees was not certain if he actually hit the fighter, but it did dive rapidly away and never returned.

On his return to base, Sergeant Rees gave a clear and fairly detailed description of both the enemy fighter and its performance. The intelligence officers were able to identify it as having been an Me 262.

Possibly even more alarming for the Allied airmen who met it in combat was the Messerschmitt Me 163 Komet. This tiny aircraft was powered by an astonishingly powerful rocket motor that produced enormous thrust, though only for a few minutes at a time. The concept was that the rocket aircraft would be launched when Allied bombers came into sight, climb rapidly to enter combat at a breathtaking 600 mph, then glide back to base when the fuel ran out. In practice they were used only against daylight raiders, which were mostly American, and so the RAF rarely encountered the Komet.

In addition to the new Luftwaffe aircraft, the by now traditional defences remained horribly effective. Radar was becoming more accurate, allowing a new searchlight system to be introduced. In each battery one searchlight, usually giving off a slightly bluish light, was controlled by short-range radar.

This master light would be directed to illuminate any radar echo. If it picked up an Allied aircraft, the rest of the searchlights would rapidly move in to cone the victim, which would then be attacked by flak or nightfighters. The flak guns now included massive 128 mm guns with a much greater range and hitting power than the already formidable 88 mm gun that had constituted German heavy flak since the war began.

The Luftwaffe nightfighters themselves were becoming more skilled and effective. Wild sow tactics had been refined by experience so that some aircraft now carried searchlights with which to illuminate victims for their comrades. Others had machine guns that fired directly upward, making it possible to rake a bomber with deadly fire while lurking safely underneath and out of reach of the bomber's gun turrets. It was as well that by 1945 a lack of aviation fuel meant that nightfighters were restricted in terms of how many hours they could fly each night.

No such problems affected the British Mosquitos that flew alongside the bombers to hunt and destroy German aircraft. On one mission over Germany in January 1945 the Mosquito piloted by Flight Lieutenant Richard Goucher, with Flight Lieutenant Charles Bullock as his observer, spotted and closed in on a Messerschmitt Me 110. They shot this aircraft down without being seen, but were not so lucky when approaching a Junkers Ju 88.

The German crew spotted the Mosquito as it approached and took immediate evasive action. There followed a high speed chase around the dark night skies of Germany between the two blacked-out aircraft. Finally Flight Lieutenant Goucher managed to let rip with a burst of cannonfire. The German aircraft exploded in a massive ball of orange flame and so close was the Mosquito that it could not avoid flying straight into the writhing mass of fire and smoke. In less than a second the British aircraft emerged back into clean air, but not without being struck by some piece of debris that caused it to lurch violently to the left and fall into a spin.

Flight Lieutenant Goucher got the aircraft under control eventually and nursed it back to level flight. The port engine was seen to be lacking its propeller, which had been torn off in the collision, while both wings were punctured by numerous holes and the paint had been scorched off in places. The aircraft was clearly not going to be able to fly for long, but Flight Lieutenant Bullock thought that they could probably make it as far as the Allied front lines in France. While Goucher gently eased the controls to keep the lone engine running and the aircraft aloft, Bullock navigated them to an airfield in France where they managed to land without further incident.

Less deadly than the Luftwaffe nightfighters, at least in the short run, were the decoy tactics carried out. Since the early days of the war, the Germans had been adept at building entirely false factories and military bases out of wood and canvas that looked very realistic from the air, particularly at night. Now they began mimicking the very Pathfinder flares that were supposed to ensure accuracy. As soon as the Pathfinders dropped their marker flares and incendiaries, the local German commander would telephone a description to a mobile unit some miles away in open countryside. They would set off identical flares and start fires, then rapidly evacuate the area. Many bombers ended up bombing open fields instead of their target. This meant that targets had to be bombed again and casualties accepted.

It was a deadly game at which the Germans were highly proficient. Fortunately the RAF too had its technical surprises and advantages. Much of this work went on under highly secretive conditions in Norfolk. At Feltwell was established the RAF Bomber Command Armaments Experimental Section, in which served Canadian Paul Brunelle. Brunelle later recalled some of his time at Feltwell:

'I joined the Permanent Royal Canadian Air Force in May 1939. As a 19-year-old trained machinist assistant, I had thought war was imminent and early enrolment wise. During my Air Armament training war was declared on 10 September 1939 and I eventually achieved a reputation as an 'innovator' Fitter Armourer. On 8 January 1945 I was seconded on loan to RAF Bomber Command to form an 'Armament Experimental Section' (AES) attached informally to the RAF Bombing Development Unit (BDU) at Newmarket racetrack, Suffolk, but BDU soon moved to RAF Feltwell, Norfolk.

'This AES group of Air Armourers was collected to apply an idea by the Bomber Command Air Armament Officer, Air Commodore Bilney, to muster and to access more efficiently the experience, skill and enthusiasms of personnel who had suggested valuable improvements. We were a Flight Sergeant, two Sergeants, two Corporals and five others, all of whom had reported to our officer-in-charge, Flight Lieutenant Badcock, RAF, by early January 1945.

'Somehow I became the NCO-in-charge and the burst of pride I felt developing, as we realized what we were expected to achieve, I feel yet, 60 years on. Flight Lieutenant Badcock, our officer-in-charge for administration, discipline and authority, wasn't much concerned with the technical aspects. I set up the daily routine as NCO-in-charge and distributed the projects to individuals or teams. We gathered almost daily for general discussions and

The RAF Bomber Command Armament Experimental Section that was based at RAF Feltwell throughout 1945. L to R back row, standing: Stan Fixter (stores), Fred Thick (stores), Jim Ilsley (guns, ballistics, ammo), Ken Morant (draughtsman), Jack Cooper (turrets and bombs), Jim Hodges (draughtsman), Bill Bosley (bomb accessories, sheet metal, woodwork); L to R middle row, sitting: Eric Schofield (mathematician, bomb accessories) 'Mac' McFarlane (mathematician, 2nd NCO i/c Section), F/Lt Badcock (officer in charge, ballistics, maths, flight, authority), Dave Williams (guns, bombs, machinist), Jeff Lord (bomb accessories, electrical, woodwork); L to R front row: Paul Brunelle (RCAF) (guns, bombs, machinist, NCO i/c Section), Chet 'Dusty' Estabrook (RCAF) (machinist, welding, i/c structures). (www.feltwell.org)

mutual help and I was informed daily of each one's progress and needs.

'This system served very well until VE Day, 8 May 1945, closed our story. Four months was too short a time for our section to really prove itself but we did accomplish a large number of fine projects. These were necessarily rough, but as safe as we could make them, produced within hours or days to solve immediate problems. Engineering and refinement came later and some may still exist.

'An example of one of our projects was the design and making of a blank firing modification of the .50 calibre Browning machine gun. This was for realistic gunner training in close quarters. I modified the barrel casing with an adjustable propulsion gas reflector on the principle of the older Vickers .303 cal. Mk V machine gun's muzzle recoil attachment. This compensated for the reduced pressure from the blank ammunition that Dave Williams had produced. He had removed the projectiles, replaced the ballistite charges with faster burning flake cordite, and crimped the necks of the rounds with a special tool he designed and made.

'Another project, done in a great hurry, was to modify the bomb bay of a Mosquito Mk XVI aircraft's bomb bay to accept a target marking bomb too large for it. We were not told why. Basically, I turned the bomb carrier sideways, but remounting that securely was very tricky.

'Bombs in a salvo jostled each other and sometimes exploded in harmony close below the bomber. The tail pistol design and its very quick arming were blamed. The eventual correction, by some other source, was an elegant modification of the existing stock of pistols by substitution of a screw type of arming fork for the nut type. We had been given this as a project and we tried several different ideas within a few days but all of them failed or were too complicated. However, by the time the new pistol showed up we had learned quite a lot.

'Our last big project was to find a way to allow tail gunners to escape from a jammed tail turret in a disabled aircraft. We weren't told so at the time, but I'm sure now that it was based on the incident in June 1944 when Sergeant Andrew Mynarski earned the Victoria Cross while trying, despite his burning clothing, to help his rear gunner to escape his jammed turret. As a team, five or six of us worked frantically on several ways to jettison the turret canopy top so that the gunner could jump upward and out. My part of this was to hinge the canopy so that, when broken away, it would leave under control, not turning inward to seriously injure the gunner.

'This was our last project and it was delivered to Bomber Command so close to VE Day that I had already received my orders to return to the RCAF for a quick trip back to Canada. There, I was to start up an Armament Experimental Section for the RCAF at Scoudouc, New Brunswick. Arriving there on 10 August 1945, I reported to the Commanding Officer who asked me for a list of what I needed to start, then to go off on thirty days of disembarkation leave. Within a couple of days of my arrival at home, VJ Day, 15 August 1945 happened, and the RCAF AES died a-borning. *Sic transit gloria.*

'Eventually I left the RCAF and returned to my former employment as a machinist, but in about three years I joined the newly formed Air Branch of the Royal Canadian Navy in which I eventually won a commission and served for about 22 years, in addition to my over six years' service in the RCAF.'

By the start of 1945 No 214 Squadron at Oulton had taken to flying American B-17 Flying Fortress aircraft. The large bombers were found to be roomier and more convenient for operating the banks of electronic equipment being used by this special duties squadron. Unfortunately the presence of a Fortress in a stream of Lancasters served to identify the aircraft to the German nightfighters as being something special, and therefore worthy of attack.

On 14 February a Fortress of No 214 Squadron was hit over Chemnitz. The intercom was destroyed and a fire started in the section of the fuselage where Sergeant Desmond Kingsland was working some of the delicate radar-jamming devices. Despite having been hit by flying debris, he managed to put the fire out before making his way forward to the pilot. Not realising that Kingsland was wounded, the pilot asked him to go around the aircraft and check to see if anyone was injured. This Kingsland did before returning to report that the only man on board who had been hit was, in fact, himself. Having been given first aid, he calmly returned to his post and continued to work for the rest of the mission.

On 7 February a No 214 Squadron Fortress was attacked by a Junkers Ju 88 nightfighter over Ladbergen. The German bullets smashed through the forward section of the bomber, destroying all the navigational equipment and seriously wounding the navigator. Sergeant Frank Hares, who was on board to work some of the more complex radar jamming equipment, had received basic training in navigation so the pilot, Flying Officer Harry Bennett, ordered him forward to assess the damage and take over.

Sergeant Hares' first task was, however, to bandage up and give painkillers to the wounded navigator. He then realised that the navigational equipment was beyond use and instead fell back on finding his way by the stars. He successfully guided the bomber back to Britain and the pilot was able to locate an emergency landing strip. By this time it was clear that the undercarriage had been damaged and that it was very likely that it would collapse on landing. This would, in turn, crush the nose of the aircraft. Hares was ordered back into the main fuselage, but he refused on the grounds that if he failed to hold the navigator still and apply pressure to his bandages, the wounded man would very likely die.

Fortunately for Sergeant Hares and the navigator the undercarriage held firm, but it was a dangerous few seconds as the bomber bounced over the turf. Sergeant Hares was given a DFM for this selfless act of mercy.

Another impressive feat of navigation took place two weeks later when a Lancaster of No 149 Squadron was hit over Witten by cannonfire from a Luftwaffe nightfighter. One engine was knocked out, the starboard wing badly damaged and the central fuselage riddled with holes. Inside the bomber both the flight engineer and pilot were wounded, the former seriously. The navigator Sergeant Kenneth Crawford, had a close escape as a cannon shell exploded inside his equipment, destroying it utterly, although he did not receive a scratch.

Sergeant Crawford attended to the wounded men before trying to get a star fix. When he failed due to heavy cloud, he fell back on dead reckoning. This involved comparing the Lancaster's heading and speed with an estimate of whatever wind might be blowing the aircraft off course. Amazingly, when the cloud cleared as he flew over the English coast, Crawford found he was only two miles from where he had estimated. The stricken bomber was able to land at Manston just a few minutes later.

Both feats, however, pale beside that of Sergeant Henry Day, a navigator in a No 462 Squadron Halifax attacking Duisberg. Over the target a flak shell exploded just above the cockpit, wounding the pilot in the head and causing him temporarily to lose his eyesight. The bomber at once fell into a steep dive at full power, from which it was rescued by the bomb-aimer, Sergeant Sydney Green. The wounded pilot could not be taken from his seat, so Green had to fly the aircraft home from an awkward standing position. This made it impossible for him to stick to a course with any success so the Halifax wandered around the sky as it headed vaguely westward toward Britain.

Sergeant Day had to undertake extremely complicated computations and measurements during this erratic flight. Not only that but he had to keep his charts and calculations constantly updated as the situation altered. He managed to guide the bomber home, for which feat his squadron commander reckoned he had to be the best navigator in Bomber Command.

As the bomber came to an emergency landing strip, Sergeant Green became increasingly worried as he began to doubt his ability to land a damaged bomber on grass at night from his position. At this point the pilot offered to retake the controls as he could now see out of his right eye. Green agreed, but stayed at the pilot's side. It was as well that he did for on the landing approach, the pilot announced that he was again losing his sight. There was

A reunion of RAF personnel and villagers, who remember them from the wartime years, held in Great Massingham church in 2005. Many locals have fond memories of the days when the RAF was a major presence in Norfolk. (Massingham MHSSLRAFMM)

no time to change hands on the controls, so Green talked the pilot down to execute a safe, if rather bumpy, landing.

An indication of how hard Bomber Command crews in Norfolk were working at this stage of the war is shown by the flight records of Sergeant Brian Butterfield, a flight engineer serving out his second tour of duty with No 635 Squadron at Downham Market. During one hectic five-night period in February, Butterfield flew sorties to Dortmund, Wuppertal, Zweibrucken, Hagen and Nuremburg.

On 16 April the government handed Harris a new and final directive. Area bombing of cities was to stop immediately. It was considered that there were quite simply no longer enough valuable targets left in German industrial cities to justify either the losses to the RAF nor the growing civilian casualties. The last attack on Berlin was carried out on 20 April 1945 by Mosquitos. Five days later a powerful force bombed Berchtesgaden in Bavaria where it was thought that Hitler and other senior Nazis might be hiding. The next night the last raid by heavy bombers struck the oil refinery at Tonsberg. Mosquitos flew in anger for the last time on 2 May when they bombed shipping in and around Kiel.

On the day that the Mosquitos were bombing Kiel, Berlin fell to the Russians. Two days later the German armies in the West surrendered to British Field Marshal Bernard Montgomery – better known simply as 'Monty'. On 7 May 1945 Germany surrendered. The war in Europe was over.

Bomber Command continued to fly missions. The most urgent of these were food drops to Holland, where areas still under German control were suffering severe food shortages and starvation. Next came shuttle flights returning prisoners of war to Britain from camps in Germany. A total of 72,500 men were brought back in just three weeks. More popular with crews were the unofficial sightseeing flights which took ground crew out to see the damage visited on Germany by the aircraft they served. For many air crews these trips were the first chance they had of seeing what they had done

The memorial that stands on the site of the long-vanished RAF Oulton.

to Germany by night. Many were shocked by the scale of the devastation and expressed amazement that Germany had continued to fight rather than collapse months earlier.

But the war was not yet over. Japan still fought on. Although it was clear that they could no longer hope to win the war, the fanatical resistance of the Japanese meant that a long and costly campaign to invade the Japanese home islands was expected to be necessary. It was scheduled to take place in early 1946. RAF Bomber Command was asked to send a force of heavy bombers to play its role in preliminary attacks on Japan and to continue to bomb the enemy once the invasion began.

This Tiger Force, as it was named, was actually in the process of being shipped out to the Far East when the atomic bombs were dropped on Nagasaki and Hiroshima in August 1945. The ships were turned around and steamed back to Britain.

For Bomber Command the war was, at last, over. The survivors could go home.

Squadron
Badges

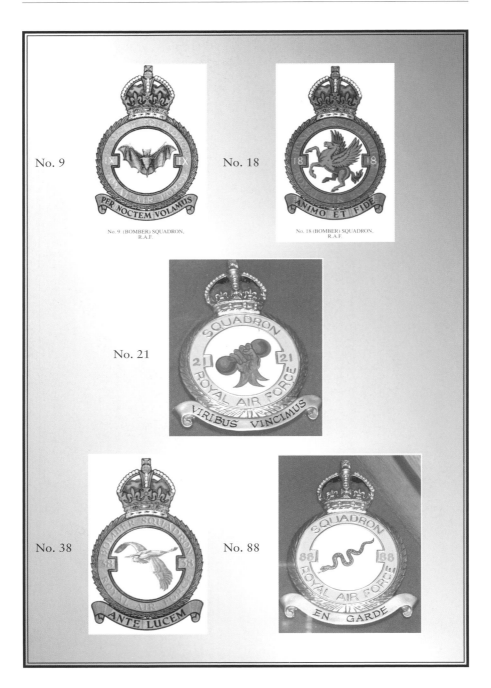

No. 9

No. 9 (BOMBER) SQUADRON,
R.A.F.

No. 18

No. 18 (BOMBER) SQUADRON,
R.A.F.

No. 21

No. 38

No. 88

No. 5

No. 114

No. 115

No. 139

No. 214

No. 236

Index

Squadrons